PETALS OF GRACE

What people are saying about *Petals of Grace*:

Beautiful! This inspirational journal teaches profound truths through everyday life occurrences or situations and drives home weighty lessons for us all.

Sola's unique perspective shows us a woman very in touch with her emotions and a child of God with a sensitive spirit who is clearly attuned to the voice of her Maker. She writes beautifully in lyric prose and poetry to encourage the reader never to give up, never mind what anyone thinks, [because] God thinks the world of you! I started reading and could not stop until I came to the very last line. Like Sola, I am an apostle of practical Christianity. No highfalutin theological musings for me, thank you! But show me love in action; and this she captures quite poignantly.

Binta Max-Gbinijie, CEO, Stanbic IBTC Trustess, Abuja, Nigeria.

Beautifully written! Using the analogy of the wonderful blessing of earthly parenthood. Sola has captured a snapshot of the eternal love of the perfect Father in this simple but beautifully written devotional. Sola invites us to experience the ever-present, ever-loving God. If you've ever wondered how much the Father loves you, *Petals of Grace* is a glimpse into that overflowing love that caused Him to give His best for you.

Bosede Santos, Speaker and Writer, Calgary, Canada,
www.bosedesantos.com

Inspirational and motivational! If you're looking for a light-hearted, uplifting devotional to start your quiet times, Sola Macaulay has provided you with just what you are looking for. This chatty, thoughtful, awesome devotional is a great way to unwind, reflect, and let God step into the day with you.

Petals of Grace is packed with entertaining real-life stories that take you into the Scriptures and help you make real-life applications. It's also a great way to start practicing the habit of looking at life through God's eyes.

Davida Yemi-Akanle, Author and Minister, London, England, http://www.davidayemiakanle.com/

Engaging and inspiring! In today's fast-paced world, it's easy to miss God's gentle whisper. Sola applies God's Word to daily living. She is a gifted writer who writes from her heart and has the ability to draw you in as she takes you on a journey of faith. So take a seat and enjoy the adventure. Each page will fill you with a longing for the lover of your soul, Christ Jesus.

Buki Ojelabi, Writer, Speaker, and Life coach, Texas, USA, http://bukiojelabi.com

PETALS OF GRACE
AN INSPIRATIONAL JOURNAL

With Compliments
Sola Macaulay Oct 2015

SOLA MACAULAY

Petals of Grace

Copyright © 2014 by Sola Macaulay

All rights reserved. No part of this publication may be reproduced, distributed, or transmitted in any form or by any means, including photocopying, recording, or any other electronic or mechanical methods, without the prior written permission of the author, except in the case of brief quotations embodied in book reviews and certain other non-commercial uses permitted by copyright law.

Unless otherwise noted, all Scripture is taken from the King James Version of the Bible. Scripture quotations marked NKJV are taken from the New King James Version®. Copyright © 1982 by Thomas Nelson, Inc., Used by permission. All rights reserved; MSG are taken from *THE MESSAGE*. Copyright © by Eugene H. Peterson 1993, 2002. Used by permission of NavPress Publishing Group; AMP are taken from the Amplified® Bible. Copyright © 1954, 1987 by The Lockman Foundation. Used by permission. (www.Lockman.org.); NIV are taken from the Holy Bible, New International Version®, NIV®. Copyright © 1973, 2011 by Biblica, Inc.™ Used by permission of Zondervan. All rights reserved worldwide. www.zondervan.com.

Paperback: ISBN 13: 978-9789436224
ISBN 10: 978943622X

Hardcover: ISBN 13: 978-978-943—621-7
ISBN 10: 9789436211

Jedidiah Publications Limited

jedidiahpubltd@gmail.com

+234-07080317274

Cover design by Damonza

Interior design by Damonza

Dedicated to you, Mum.

Princess Christie Olufunmilayo Ashiru-Suinner
1947–2014

I had hoped you'd be here when I published my first book. I remember the words you spoke about my writing.—an inspiring and encouraging word at a time when I didn't foresee myself pushing through the mountain of doubts. A few hours after you took your last breath, God dropped it in my spirit to begin work on this book. Well, here I am, Mum. Doing what you saw into the future, doing exactly what God has called me to do.

*Like blooming spring flowers, your grace is fresh,
lovely, tender, fragrant and colorful.*

(Adapted from Songs of Solomon 2:12 MSG)

TABLE OF CONTENTS

Preface xiii
Acknowledgments. xv
Foreword xvii
Of Love, Hope, and Trust. 1
    One: And the Rhyme Goes 3
    Two: The Only Constant in a Changing World. 6
    Three: Again, I Love You. 9
    Four: Dandled on His Knees 11
    Five: Just One More Try. 14
    Six: He Loves Me; He Loves Me Not 17
    Seven: Invisible. 20
    Eight: I Love You; I Died for You 23
    Nine: Help from the Gutters 26
Of Purpose, Waiting, and Character 29
    One: Fried Ice Cream. 31
    Two: Don't Mess with My Mind. 34
    Three: God's Oxymoron. 37
    Four: Good People Are Still in the Land 41
    Five: Restoration Rights 44
    Six: Do You Decaf?. 48
    Seven: E Not Your Own, E My Own 51
    Eight: Wasted Spaces 53
    Nine: One Hundred KM/H 55
    Ten: Detoxify Me, Puhleeze 60

Eleven: You Can Tame the Growl 65

Twelve: I Must Restock Quickly 68

Thirteen: Naïve. 71

Fourteen: Waves and Wonder 75

Fifteen: Switch to the End 78

Sixteen: Dangerous Mission 81

Seventeen: Numbers & Stats. 84

Eighteen: Foundations 88

Nineteen: What If? 91

Twenty: Beauty and Glory 94

Twenty-One: Ordinary people 99

Twenty-Two: Composting the Dead 102

Twenty-Three: A Little Mud and Spit 105

Twenty-Four: The Pupa Party 108

Of Redemption, Restoration, and Worship 111

One: Ugly Is Beautiful 113

Two: Approved for Travel 116

Three: The Gentle Crooner. 119

Four: Speed 123

Five: A Prison Break at Christmas 128

Six: Change? No, Not Me 132

Seven: Tilt to the Light 134

Eight: The Squall 136

Nine: My Name in Neon Lights 139

Ten: Have You Met My Son? 141

Eleven: TLC 143

Before You Go 147

Afterword 149

PREFACE

WHEN I WROTE the first article that is now included in *Petals of Grace*, I had no idea I would be writing to publish. A series of experiences and observations drove me to the pen. I decided to share my musings by creating a blogging platform. After two years of writing, I felt an inner nudge to reach for a wider audience.

By wider audience I modestly thought it meant getting more traffic to my blog or getting a Website, applying the many online marketing strategies. God, however, had a different plan. He instructed me to edit, rewrite, and format these collections into an easy-to-read book.

Although I had never published a book, I presumed my first book would be the fiction I've been crafting for the past five years. I didn't think writing a book like this would make any marketing sense, especially not enough to build an author profile.

Despite my misgivings, I obeyed God and began to organize the articles.. I have enjoyed every moment of getting inspired while writing this book. What you will read in the next pages I pray will be exactly what God wants you to read, to know, and to rediscover about Him. Amen.

The purpose of *Petals of Grace* is to help you see God in everyday situations, help you ask questions about how God operates in our lives, and help you see and accept that in all situations God remains unfailingly loving and worthy of worship and adoration.

We are here for a definite purpose. Once we discover that purpose, how do we live the Christian life within it, with a redemptive future in mind? Some of the articles are biographical; some are theological; most are inspirational, witty, and humorous; and the rest can be deemed philosophical musings.

Today people ask: Where is God when I'm hurting? Where is God when I'm down? I have asked the same questions time and again, but I have been satisfied with the ways God came through for me. The best moments in life have been those times when I learned to let go and trust God completely.

I pray that you draw closer to God as you take this journey with me live in my world, feel my pain, and share in the laughter around my life. I pray mostly that God will show up not just in your situation but also in your personal life. I pray that you have an awesome encounter with this God of the universe we serve. When your heart feels lighter, when a smile tugs as the corners of your mouth, and when your thoughts of God run deeper, then my job is done.

Welcome to this journey with our awesome God.

I pray that like *Petals of Grace*, God's love will make your life beautiful, colorful, and fragrant.

Blessings,
Sola Macaulay
Lagos, Nigeria
December 2014

ACKNOWLEDGMENTS

TO MY HUSBAND, Kofoworola. You believed in me through the years and always called me your maverick. You loved me through it all; the years of waiting, the pints of blood you gave, the endless sacrifices to me, our families and to many others. You're a treasure, my treasure. Thank you for sticking with me through the journey. You're my 'gentleman', my friend, and the many beats in my heart. Love you to the stars and back.

To my daughter, Oluwatofunmi, my little princess. You're a breath of fresh air, the arrow in our quiver, our child of promise. You often talked about Petals of Grace, asking to help Mummy write the book. You're the inspiration behind many of the articles in this book. Mummy loves you very much!

To my siblings, George Honey & Remi Ashiru, Lola & Bimbo Olaide-Stephen, Kate Suinner, Feigne Suinner, and Anne Titi & Dele Lawoyin, I couldn't have asked for better siblings. You guys rock! Love you to bits.

To my dad, Abbey O. Ashiru, you're always just a phone call away, ready and willing to listen to my endless ramblings. You always cheered me up. Love you, Dad.

To my Grandmother, Chief Mrs. R. Ola Osunsanmi, who is more like my second mum; for your constant prayers, love and for being my greatest cheerleader. Maami!

To my in-laws, Chief and Chief Mrs. C.A.O. Macaulay, for loving me like your own daughter.

To my second siblings: Doye & Barbara Macaulay, Seni & Toks

Macaulay, Ronke Macaulay and Tunde & Kemi Macaulay, for being this wonderful to your sister-in-law.

To my friend and mentor, Oluremi Bendega—what can I say about your friendship? Priceless! Thank you for your prayers, for encouraging me through the years and for always being there for me.

To my friend and sister, Olufunmi Olajoyegbe—with you, friendship is so real, so fun and so valuable. Thank you for the many chats, tears and laughter.

To Pastors Taiwo and Nomthi Odukoya, for the seeds you have sown in my life and for being an exceptionally good example of a Christian. God bless you!

To my writing buddies, I salute you all for the courage to forge ahead and leave the trail burning for the rest of us: Sinmisola Ogunyinka, Bola Essien-Nelson, Unyime Ivy-King, and Abimbola Dare.

To Ola Nubi, winner of Wasafiri International Prize For Fiction, 2009. You don't know how the many chats we had on Facebook inspired me to take the first step. You encouraged me every time to live my dream and get published. Thank you!

To my editor, Erin Brown, for a fantastic editing job ironing out all the kinks and transforming this book into an easy flow read. Thumbs up, Lady!

And to my loving Father, the only wise God, my Savior, my Redeemer, my Friend, the lover of my soul and the giver of every gift I have; Lord, I am deeply and eternally grateful for all you've done in my life. I am grateful for the journey behind and the journey ahead. You have demonstrated Your love for me as though there was only me to love. Thank You, Jesus! I love You with every breath in me.

FOREWORD

I MET SOLA Macaulay about seventeen years ago while I was head of the Bible College of a leading Pentecostal church here in Lagos-Nigeria. In the course of time, our families got closer, and our relationship has deepened over the years. One thing I discovered about Sola is her hunger for God—her strong desire to know more of God and to do His will. She is passionate about life and about her faith. Even though unassuming and quiet, she is very deep.

Petals of Grace is a masterpiece. I had no dull moments going through it. The content is both rich and substantial. Even though Christian, it is not the typical religious book that ostracizes readers of other religions. It contains something for everyone—the discouraged, the frustrated, the fallen, the confused, the skeptic . . . you name it.

I found it profound, piercing, thought provoking, sobering, and inspiring. The encouraging, instructive, and motivational content of this book qualifies it as a compendium for life. So captivating is the style of presentation that, once I started reading it, I could not put it down but read until the last page. I broke down and wept while reading certain portions. At other times, I shuddered at the greatness and awesomeness of God. Other portions sent me looking inward and pondering deeply about my life and about my relationship with other people, with God, and with eternity. *Petals of Grace* is a reference book for life, one I would love to return to again and again in the remaining years of my earthly sojourn because of the timeless truths and the weighty instructions in it.

I highly recommend this book to everyone in need of motivation, inspiration, revival, restoration, and encouragement.

William Ukpada Bendega
Minister, Omega House, Lagos, Nigeria

OF LOVE, HOPE, AND TRUST

I HAVE HAD sincere moments when I doubted God's love. Moments when all hope seemed lost and I didn't think I could trust God again. Thankfully, they were transient moments.

God never leaves us comfortless. His message to us is a message of love, confirmed time and time again in the Bible, from Genesis to Revelation. I found these verses comforting and I hope you do too.

Herein is love, not that we loved God, but that he loved us, and sent his Son to be the propitiation for our sins.

1 John 4:10

We love him, because he first loved us.

1 John 4:19

For we are saved by hope.

Romans 8:24a

Be of good courage, and he shall strengthen your heart, all ye that hope in the LORD.

Psalm 31:24

What time I am afraid, I will trust in thee.

Psalm 56:3

They that trust in the LORD shall be as mount Zion, which cannot be removed, but abideth for ever.

Psalm 125:1

ONE
AND THE RHYME GOES...

It's raining, it's pouring,
The old man is snoring.
We read the book and sang the song
While it rains all night long.

IT'D BEEN FUN reading nursery rhymes again and again with my effervescent toddler.

One day when it began to rain, she looked up. She'd never been in the rain before. From the eager look on her face and before I had a chance to explain to her what to expect, she took off in the direction of the back door, bounded down the short steps, and ran smack-dab into the onslaught of the heavy downpour.

The shock of cold water on her body thrilled her. She squealed! Her clothes and new hairdo became immediately soaked. We ran upstairs to get something more appropriate for her to wear in the rain. We yanked off clothes, nappy, and shoes. Not an easy feat with a wriggling, slippery toddler. Once she'd donned her swim costume, she sped back into the wet world.

I stood watching her yell and scream, "Mummy! Weeee!"

It filled my heart with pride and joy to see her having a blast. She had no cares in the world. Just enjoying nature's gift.

It brought back many memories.

Memories of days when things were simpler, you know, days when we were young and had no complicated thoughts. No convoluted ideas. No pretenses, ulterior motives, or sinister diplomacy. People were simply who they were: people. Not necessarily rivals or archenemies.

There's something special about children—something pristine, pure, and true. No wonder Jesus compared receiving the kingdom of God much like little children. And Jesus said to them, 'Yes. Have you never read, "Out of the mouth of babes and nursing infants You have perfected praise"'" (Matt. 21:16 nkjv); "Whoever receives one of these little children in My name receives Me; and whoever receives Me, receives not Me but Him who sent Me" (Mark 9:37 nkjv); "But when Jesus saw it, He was greatly displeased and said to them, 'Let the little children come to Me, and do not forbid them; for of such is the kingdom of God'" (10:14 nkjv).

The heart of faith doesn't get entangled in philosophical questions about the Word of God. God's love for us is what draws us close. The understanding of that love inspired by His Word enriches and increases our faith. It's not that complicated, really.

My daughter's scream of pain brought me out of my reverie. I dropped my camera and rushed to catch her, but I could not reach her in time. She'd slipped and fallen; yet she still ran into my arms for comfort. After having received my comfort and kisses on her forehead and cheeks, like, a zillion times, she headed out again into the rainstorm.

God reaches out to us in love. He doesn't just want to wrestle us from the entanglement of sin and the Devil; He wants to love us for eternity. The thought of that thrills and fills me with awe.

My daughter loves me, but I first loved her before she knew who I was. God loved me long before I knew and loved Him too.

Awesome!

We finally had to drag my daughter in from the rain, give her a hot shower, and keep her warm. Next time I'm going to let my hair down and join her in the rain. How about that?

PONDER THIS:

Do you sometimes wish you could trash all of your problems in a burner and just let your hair down? Well, why don't you?

TWO
THE ONLY CONSTANT IN A CHANGING WORLD

I trust you, Lord,
More than I trust the sun to shine.
I trust you, Lord,
More than I trust even time.
I trust you, Lord,
Even if the earth shifts.
Your love is my ever-constant world.

THE HORNS BLARED and I knew my daughter would come running from the school bus and into the house. Typically, I would receive her at the front door with a hug, but at that moment I was composing an important email and filling out an online questionnaire. So I had someone else open the door for her.

I looked up briefly, expecting her excited chatter to filter through the door. Instead, I heard a door slam and an ensuing hush. I ignored my gut feeling and resumed my email, trusting she would ultimately join me.

I did not expect the wail that sliced through the silent house—the mummy-labeled wail that could get me scuttling to her in an instant. I took in a deep breath and walked to where she remained at the door, not having taken another step into the house.

She stood there sobbing!

I pulled her into my arms, rubbing her back while trying to figure out what went wrong. From the dried tears on her cheeks, to the down-turned mouth and the crushed paper toy, I guessed I'd doused her excitement. She must have planned to show me her toy bird.

I later learned she had been holding it up, expecting I would be the one to meet her, but seeing someone else at the door changed all that. I apologized and explained to her that I loved her, but I may not always be there to meet her at the door.

In that instant, I sensed the Lord switching my emotions with my daughter's until I understood how she felt. In a split second, I could not imagine calling on God and meeting cold silence. I could not imagine ascending the throne of grace and not finding help. I could not imagine calling the name of Jesus and not seeing the mountains shift.

I could not imagine longing for the presence of His sweet Spirit and finding Him too busy for me. Oh no! I just could not imagine it.

These were things I expect because God's Word assures me of His help in my time of need.

Yet for my daughter in the moment, when I was not there to meet her at the usual time, she felt abandoned, not given priority.

For now I was her world. In a short while that would change and she would outgrow the dependency.

I'm glad we don't outgrow dependency on God. In fact, we cannot survive without total and unreserved dependency on God and His Word.

For a finite lover of my daughter, we both had to come to terms with the fact that I won't always be there for her, even though that's my desire. But for the infinite lover of my soul, I needn't worry that I could not reach Him whenever I called.

He is always here for us. Always. When we betray Him, He is here. When we hurt Him, He remains steadfast. When we shun Him, crucify Him afresh, willfully sin against Him, He remains constant, ever loving and waiting for us to come back home.

God specializes in being the one to welcome us. He doesn't send a second-in-command, a host of angels, or a welcoming committee. No! He personally comes running to us, to welcome us, just as the father did the prodigal son. He saw the prodigal son from afar and ran toward him.

God is the only one who never changes, whose Word is His bond, a resounding yea and amen. He is constant and always here, but we are not. We can only grasp Him now or miss Him for eternity.

Time changes. You and I change. Life passes on. Today might be your day of salvation. Will you grasp Him?

Consider these verses: "We then, as workers together with Him also plead with you not to receive the grace of God in vain. . . . In an acceptable time I have heard you, and in the day of salvation I have helped you. Behold, now is the accepted time; behold, now is the day of salvation" (2 Cor. 6:1–2 nkjv).

"What time I am afraid, I will trust in thee" (Ps. 56:3).

"For I am the *Lord*, I change not" (Mal. 3:6a).

Ponder This:

Have you ever doubted God's constant love for you? Has He ever failed to make the sun shine?

THREE
AGAIN, I LOVE YOU

A tickle, a giggle, a sigh
Are life's little pleasures
Found in the place of mirth
Before the presence of the One
In whom even joy delights.

THE CLOUDS WERE a dark grey when I left home to pick up my daughter from school. It was swim day, so I knew she'd had fun.

My busy day had worn me out. Workmen had been in and out of the house fixing this and that. On top of that, my allergies had flared, but I couldn't rest because I had so much to do.

I picked up my daughter. We strode down the road, headed home. Halfway through our journey, the sky opened and poured down its fury. My puny little umbrella didn't hold up against the onslaught. My daughter clung to me and I held what was left of the umbrella over her head to at least shield her hair. The rest of our bodies felt the wrath of the downpour. Hugging her tight against my chest, I trudged on in the pouring rain, my long skirt dragging muddy water about me.

We got home soaked, cold, and exhausted. I quickly grabbed some towels and rubbed down my daughter, gave her something hot to drink, and switched on the heater. She ate some dry toast while watching TV as I tidied the house. She was thrilled when I stepped into the shower with her a few minutes later.

Having a shower together made her scream with delight. As her soft giggle bounced around the bathroom, contentment filled me. I chose to forget the inconvenience of not having a car yet while still trying to manage our life until things settled down a bit. Spending time with her was my own way of saying "I love you." Her excited chatter was her way of responding "I love you too."

Sometimes life charges in like a ferocious bull or a thunderous downpour, but you only have to take a second look around you to see the little blessings God has bestowed on you. Spending time with my daughter and hearing her giggle and watching her play made my day. My weariness subsided, and I forgot all about what I had or didn't have.

No matter how dark it is, a flicker of light is always somewhere: a swaying flower to remind you of life's beauty; a glorious sunset; warm, sandy beaches; chirping birds; a gentle smile; a phone call or email from a friend; a playful joke; or a surprise package.

These are all life's little pleasures and God's way of saying "I love you." "Then was our mouth filled with laughter, and our tongue with singing: then said they among the heathen, The Lord hath done great things for them" (Ps. 126:2); "We love him, because he first loved us" 1 John 4:19).

Ponder This:

Do you slow down long enough to notice the little pleasures of life, like the taste of cool water on a thirsty tongue? Have you noticed many others? You should.

FOUR
DANDLED ON HIS KNEES

I love your tender mercies
I love that you never change
I love your thoughts of me
I love that you love me so
I love that You are the definition of love

"**MUMMY!**"

My daughter's scream reached me while I was in the bathroom. I didn't wait for business to finish. I wrapped it up, almost half clad, flew down the stairs, not caring for my safety, and sped out to where the cry came from.

It's the cry every mother both anticipates and dreads. It doesn't matter where I am or what I am doing, once she cries, I'm all out.

I was in the bathroom when the Lord dropped this inspiring article on me—the ideas often come in the weirdest places and at the most unusual times. It makes me realize that God has the best sense of humor. You know, I believe the bathroom is one place you can't rush business. That's also one place my mind isn't always roaming, because I'm concentrating hard on getting on with business, and then *wham*, God drops something in my spirit. Totally out of whack!

Well, back to the outcry. I sped out of the house to rescue my daughter from whatever was causing her distress. I discovered that her outcry was just the result of an argument she'd had with her nanny.

It's amazing how oftentimes her anguish is a result of only a minor incident, scrape, or disagreement with her nanny. When she cries "Mummy!" like Superwoman, with a flowing red cape, I run, or dare I say fly, to the rescue. That's how much I love my children. I protect them fiercely from harm and danger.

I remember one night while getting ready to pray. As soon as my knees hit the floor I said, "Father."

Yes, daughter, the Lord responded.

Wow! I was taken aback. It wasn't what I expected. We typically pray and just believe in faith that God hears us, yet in the back of our minds, we think He's busy having a conference with the angels about some big shot on the mission field and would get back to little ol' us later. We expect a response, an answer to our prayers, but we honestly don't anticipate an instant answer. That's because God wants us to live by faith. So says the Bible in Mark 11:24, that when you pray, believe, right?

That was my attitude. I did believe, I just didn't expect an answer so soon. But every once in a while, God steps out of eternity into our little worlds and interrupts the balance of normalcy.

That night I was amazed, to say the least. I was both so excited and surprised by God's quick response that I failed to utter another word. I didn't know what to say. That wasn't the time to be eloquent—to recite perfectly memorized scriptures or a mode of liturgy.

What do you do when God speaks? Do you try to impress Him, or demand a long-standing request?

I'd rather be awed by His love, to bask in His presence and let His love fill me to overflowing. In a nutshell, I'd rather be dandled on His knees.

I hear in my spirit His words in Isaiah 49:15, "Can I forget my suckling child?" Rhetorical question or not, I know that I could never forget my daughter. So God says He, even more, can *never* forget me.

Because I love my daughter, I may be quick to rescue her. But sometimes I may not rush to her side, because in leaving her to face certain things, I'm helping her to grow strong and mature. How much more does

God to this for us. I can't imagine moments of not caring for my child, yet when she drives me batty, I have a few words for her.

God says in His Word that He can never forget us nor stop loving us, even when we do the most stupid and seemingly unforgivable things. He compares His love for us with the love of a nursing mother. A nursing mother's love is delicate, passionate, and fiercely protective. God says He loves us deeper and much more than that. Wow! "The Lord has appeared of old to me, saying: 'Yes, I have loved you with an everlasting love; Therefore with lovingkindness I have drawn you.'" (Jer. 31:3 nkjv).

And I really love this translation from *The Message* Bible: "God told them, 'I've never quit loving you and never will. Expect love, love, and more love!'"

Regardless of how you feel or what your status is in life, it doesn't change this: God's love is perfect and everlasting.

Wouldn't you want to be dandled on His knees?

Ponder This:

Have you ever wished you could be a child again and God dandles you on His knees? Be that child on the inside. That simplicity is endearing to God.

FIVE
JUST ONE MORE TRY

A little more time,
A little more try,
A little step forward,
A little to the left,
Or even to the right,
Might reveal a nugget
Hidden from mere sight.

I DESPERATELY NEEDED A boost of cash. I had a little emergency and saw no other way out except to visit an ATM.

ATMs were not plentiful in residential areas like ours, so I crossed my fingers, hoping the three or four lined on the main street would have available cash. The only other option would be to drive the long distance to the commercial area, but my fuel gauge was dangerously low.

I tried the first cash machine, but it was out of cash. I drove a few blocks and tried the next one. It didn't accept Visa cards. Great! Just two more to go. I drove to the next one, and the guard said the machine was out of order. Aaargh! One more try. I entwined my fingers tightly. I needed more than crossed fingers; I needed a miracle.

A pocket of traffic, which was unusual for the time of day that Sunday, slowed me down. I was getting frustrated and running out of time and options. I switched off the air-conditioner to save fuel. My daughter fidgeted and whined about the heat. My heart beat fast as we approached the last one. I muttered a prayer and walked toward the machine. Two people stood ahead of me. I was excited that at least this ATM worked. I asked the man before me if the machine accepted Visa. He nodded. I beamed and felt lighthearted.

After the last man got his cash and left, I slotted my card in and punched in my pin and other details. As I waited for the machine to count my cash, the dispensing slot beeped a few times, as though it was about to expel the cash, then it stopped. The error message that flashed on the screen felt like hammer beating on my head: Out of Cash.

At that moment, the conflicting emotions of anger and frustration ran through me. On the verge of tears I stood speechless. I had exhausted all the available machines. I hadn't any more fuel to drive anywhere else except home. I needed the cash desperately.

"Lord, what am I supposed to do now?" I pray as tears trickled down my cheeks

I sat in the car and rested my head on the dashboard, wondering what next. I decided to go back home. It was better than being stuck outside without any cash or fuel. I put the car in reverse and looked in the rearview mirror. And that's when I saw it—an obscure ATM signpost. It pointed to a corner street.

With baited breath and my heart pounding, I drove down the street and found a lonely ATM in the middle of nowhere. I almost drove off, thinking such an unmanned machine couldn't have cash, but curiosity got the better of me. So I held my breath and tried. I slipped in my card and entered my information. The machine beeped . . . and belched out crisp notes! I was torn between shouting and laughing.

Often at the point when we're about to give up, God urges us to take one more step, just one more try. It could be you've tried all you know to do, and you're about to give up. Just try again, just one more step. You're closer to your miracle than you think. Just one more try, one more step, one more push is all you need.

Don't give up just yet. You're closer than you imagine.

"Trust in the Lord with all your heart, and lean not on your own understanding; In all your ways acknowledge Him, and He shall direct your paths" (Prov. 3:5–6 nkjv).

Ponder This:

Have you ever almost given up on something or someone? Give a little more grace, won't you?

SIX
HE LOVES ME; HE LOVES ME NOT

God's love
Is not to be trifled with.
God's love
Is not to be doubted.
God's words
Are the assurances we need.
For God's love
Is ours, everlasting.

LATELY, ONE OF the critical things the Lord has been teaching me is His singular love for us. It is important to be so secure in this love that nothing can sway us.

We are neither prone to be in dire need of nor disillusioned about the reassurance that somebody loves us.

Have you ever asked: Where were all the folks Jesus healed when He was being testified against? Where was the man with the withered hand? Where were the others: the blind, the lame, the sick, and the dead who rose from the grave? Where were they when the crowd chose Barabbas to be released instead of Jesus? Okay, they were at home interceding for Pilate to make the right decision? Right, let's leave that for now.

Granted, Jesus didn't rely so much on the cheers and love of the crowd. He knew the hearts of men. At the garden of Gethsemane, He went for all night prayers with eleven of His disciples. One had opted out. He then chose Peter, James, and John to go farther in with Him. Three times He came back to rouse His disciples from sleep. At the end of the day, it had to be Him alone. The Bible says an angel strengthened Him.

To be honest, I don't see how the disciples would have been able to stay up praying, let alone with the intensity with which Jesus prayed. Blame the frailties of the human nature without endowment from on high. Every now and then, we will go to our own Gethsemane, where it will just be us and God.

This is where we have to be secure in God's love. Like the song says, "The steadfast love of the Lord *never* ceases."

When you are sheltered in God's love, you can face almost anything, because you're constantly reminded that God loves you endlessly, and He makes all things work together for your benefit and good.

Let's not play "he loves me; he loves me not" with God. God Himself is the personification of love.

I'm in a season in which God is teaching me about His love. He is blowing my mind to smithereens with demonstrations of His love. He is teaching me more about the security found in His perfect love, not the gushing emotions and having material and physical things that make one feel loved. I want to grow up and move from feeling loved to knowing I am loved. His love is much more tangible than the things we see with our eyes.

Getting back to the Barabbas and Gethsemane saga, did it bother Jesus that the same people He healed, delivered, and set free testified against Him? The Bible records that the love God the Father had for Jesus had such a great impact that He could love us still. Did the Father love Jesus less when He sent Him to the cross? We can't measure God's love by only the material benefits we gain. Neither ought we to doubt His love by the adversities we face.

God's love is constant, regardless of what we do or don't do. We need to be mega secure in His love, such that adversity pales in comparison. In eternity we will, I suppose, fully grasp the extent of God's love. But for now, you and I should just hold on to and trust the God who holds eternity in His grasp.

PONDER THIS:

Have you ever felt betrayed by people you trusted? Jesus felt this pain too, yet He stayed loving.

SEVEN
INVISIBLE

The silver thread
That weaves the rungs
Of our lives,
He inserts
Into the fabrics
Of our beings.
Every needlepoint
He grafts
With caring eyes
And gentle hands.

HAVE YOU EVER felt invisible? You know, like the whole world is spinning in all of its glory and totally oblivious to your existence. The feeling that you don't really matter. That feeling that there is and will always be others more important than you?

As a child I was plagued by the thought that I would walk this earth and pass into eternity without anyone knowing I existed. That's a weird phobia for a child, the dread of insignificance.

Why did I feel this way? Is it because I was extremely introverted? Talking was a hassle for me, and I found social activity draining. Introverts or melancholic people draw energy from other people and the environment.

That's our mainstay energy depot. We churn this energy boost and convert it to creative leanings. We don't use energy just to chat and hangout.

So how does one who is so buried in ideas and concepts make impactful achievements in the big wide world? Very easy! Have a target audience.

Although I've read Tim LaHaye's *Spirit-Controlled Temperament*, one day many years ago my temperament style ceased to matter. Choleric or Melancholy, God can use anyone. Jesus's disciples were a good mix of the temperaments, but on the day of Pentecost, personality type wasn't a factor. These men were filled with boldness and they shook the world. That's the Holy Spirit for you.

Then again, what makes you feel invisible? That you're not famous, rich, accomplished, . . . or what? When the Holy Ghost comes upon you, the issue of invisibility vanishes. God will empower you to be and accomplish what He has specifically called you to do, which nobody else can do quite the way He has equipped you to do it. How does that count for being invisible when the God of the universe reckons you usable?

By all means, strive to accomplish something. We all pursue vocations, and we should strive for excellence in all we do. But never ever feel limited by your shortcomings or believe you are invisible because your name is not in neon lights or in big bold print. Remind yourself that "When the Holy Spirit comes," everything changes. Remember Genesis 1? Everything was invisible. Nothing had a shape or form. It was all a chaotic nothingness until word came from headquarters and the Holy Spirit moved.

When you've been through rough seasons and now it's time for you to rise, *nothing* can stop you when the Spirit of Grace comes. Even now, you're not invisible. You may be in a waiting room until your time of showing. What counts is whom you're visible to—God. God should be your target audience.

You can't be invisible to the One who loves you enough to die for you. He knew when you arrived on this side of eternity, He knew what you would accomplish, He knew your joys and pain, He knew the number of strands of hair on your head, and He knows when you will rejoin Him on the other side of eternity. How does that make you invisible? Don't stress to be visible to finite beings. Let God be your target audience and He will choose where to place you. If you're looking for a place to be famous, choose heaven first. Do they know you in heaven? Do even the demons know you and tremble? Aha!

The day you arrive in heaven, *all* of heaven will rejoice. You will be visible where it counts the most.

When God said in Isaiah 49:16, "I have engraved you on the palm of my hands," He was talking specifics. Specifically, you. Not an invisible, inconsequential, unimportant being. He was talking about you, whom He lovingly made.

Ponder This:

Never mind what anyone thinks of you. God thinks the world of you.

EIGHT
I LOVE YOU; I DIED FOR YOU

His death is the language
That life gave to me.
His pain is the whisper
Health spoke to me.
His word is the language
That love sang to me.

GIVEN THAT I write often, I don't plan ahead what I will write. When I am inspired, I just write. However, I was given specific instructions for what I'm about to share with you.

I'd wrestled with some long-standing challenges that seemed to go on and on. I'd been through various seasons in my life in which I learned, and I think I understood a little, about waiting on God.

Nothing ever comes easy.

The good bit is that when God comes through, it's usually in a mind-blowing way. I don't mind waiting for God. Every wait is worth it.

But this particular issue was so mind-boggling; it rattled the very foundation of my faith. For the second time in my faith walk, I questioned God. Oh, I knew His Word, had seen Him come through for me on numerous occasions, and I had never been disappointed with the outcome. But, truth be told, I displayed my humanity and balked. I consoled myself that even Paul, even with all his anointing, could not pray off his thorn in his flesh.

There are just some things God's sovereignty holds sway over. It's not lack of faith but God's wisdom at work.

Like I said, this issue drove me to my knees and to tears. I hardly ever cry. Women do, yes, but I don't routinely let the tears flow . . . until this challenge reminded me of the crying option. I felt gut-wrenching pain engulf my heart. Torrents of tears flooded my eyes and tumbled down my cheeks. I not only cried, I moaned and groaned. I couldn't help it. It's okay to cry. In fact, it helps a great deal. Yet I didn't get any relief. The longer I cried, the deeper the pain went.

It wasn't the cry of "Oh Lord, why me?" It was the cry of "Wish it wouldn't hurt so much." I could go through almost anything as long as it didn't involve emotional pain or mental anguish. Depravity, yes, but not internal pain, where absolutely no one and nothing but God could reach and fix.

Through my swollen eyes and dampened spirit, I decided to be real with God. "Lord, I don't mind tests. I know You won't let me face more than I can bear, but why did it have to hurt so much?" I didn't wait for an answer but kept giving in to the groans and sobs.

Then something unexpectedly happened that I'd never experienced before. I heard His voice singing these words in my spirit: *I love you; I gave My life to save you.*" This song went on for a while. I was stupefied, excited, confused, elated, uplifted. I mean, I knew God would speak to me through His Word, deposit a thought in my spirit, speak through His people and circumstances, but I'd never heard Him speak to me not just through a song but also with a song into my spirit.

In that moment, I compared my pain to the pain on the cross. The agony my sinless Savior had to bear for me. My pain was nowhere near what Jesus went through at Calvary. And here was God reminding me that He loved me in spite of my pain. That He loved me in spite of whatever I was going through. The balance had always been tipped in my favor. The cross versus my finite, temporary pain; how could they ever compare?

You can't put God in a box. No! Not in a million years. That song did it for me. It settled in my spirit and settled me. I wept even more, but now tears of joy and appreciation filled me to overflowing. It moved me into a deeper worship zone. I think for the rest of my life I will always remember, in a personal way, that God loves me eternally. He gave me His most precious gift: Jesus. Jesus loves me, gave His life for me, and did not leave me without comfort. The Holy Spirit lives in me to ratify and make that love real to me.

Normally, I would write this incident in my private journal, since it's my personal experience. But the Lord instructed me to write an article about it. Here's what He told me:

Write it down. Make it plain. Write it down for all to see, so that the world may know how much I love you and _____ [put your name on the line]. *Signed, God.*

PONDER THIS:

I have played my part and now ask the question: Do you know that God loves you unconditionally? He loves you too much to let you die in your sins. The unconditional is predicated on the premise of the condition that you repent to fully embrace all of Him.

NINE
HELP FROM THE GUTTERS

When I seek for the Lord's help,
I often think of how He should come through,
Thinking of ways and vessels He could use,
Forgetting that He sees far beyond
The little road ahead of me.
When I sit still and let Him drive my life,
He sends help just the way I need it.

I WAS MINDING MY business, enjoying an early morning, brisk walk in a bid to keep fit. The crisp cool air and Harmattan dust settled over the street.

I picked up a few groceries along the way.

On the way home, clutching two full shopping bags, I spotted two women in sweat suits jogging. It was nice to see people trying to keep fit. Then I noticed three young men sitting and chatting in front of an uncompleted building on the opposite side of the street as I passed by. I wondered what they were discussing so early in the morning and why they were not busy doing something worthwhile.

I could see my house in the distance and decided to climb up the pavement. I took maybe two or three steps before the world went wobbly and I lunged forward. That was when I fully understood the laws of gravity and why it didn't favor me, especially when I was wearing a long skirt.

If I could command gravity to stand still, believe me, I would have in an instant. Maybe a new she-Joshua would emerge. But, alas, I wasn't going to be named she-Joshua that day.

I pushed one foot in front of the other in an attempt to steady myself, but it didn't work. The only thing that worked was the inevitable. I fell on the concrete; my shopping bags burst and belched their contents all over the street. My Nokia phone (thank God for Nokia) spilled its guts. I lay spread-eagle on the ground.

The shock of my fall zipped through my system like an electric current, and my first thought was, "What kind of nonsense fall is this!"

The view from the ground wasn't pretty. How do I get up and regain my dignity? The truth was I couldn't get up. Imagine!

One of the young men I'd just passed came to my rescue. He reached for my right hand and pulled me up, and then he helped me gather my things that had scattered on the ground. My hands shook as I tried to retrieve and fix my phone. The jogging women across the street called out in sympathy. I looked up at the chap and thanked him profusely. If he hadn't helped me up, I don't know how long I would have had to stay like that until I swallowed my pride and asked for help.

Falling down is common to children, but it's not as traumatic for them because they are lighter and smaller. But the saying is true: The bigger they are the harder they fall. So when an adult like me falls from what seems a zillion feet to the ground, it calls for swallowing your pride and screaming for help.

You never know how help can come and through whom. This chap helped me at such a bizarre incident, even though I had judged him and his friends as layabouts. I believe God placed them there to help me when I needed it. Don't thrust your source of help away because of the packaging. God can use anybody, anything, and any situation to help in times of need.

I mustered up the shreds of dignity I had left, held my chin up, and walked the rest of the journey home. This was not the time to be embarrassed. I considered a couple of verses: "Make haste to help me, O Lord my salvation" (Ps. 38:22); and "God is our refuge and strength, a very present help in trouble" (46:1).

God can use anything and absolutely anyone to reach you, to help you. Never mind about the package. It's the contents that matter most.

Ponder This:

Have you ever disdained someone because he or she didn't quite fit your ideas and ideals? You possibly limit God when you do. Please don't. God sees far beyond the surface.

OF PURPOSE, WAITING, AND CHARACTER

Waiting on God is a tough call. Waiting with a clear purpose is rewarding. Living a life of purpose builds our character over time. Character is the reward of diligently living a life that pleases God. But it all takes time. However, once we understand our purpose, it makes waiting a little easier, and perhaps we can more easily see the meaningfulness of it all.

In the next few pages, I have shared my thoughts and experiences that demonstrate my frustrations, shortcomings, and little victories of purpose, waiting, and character.

> *But those who wait upon God get fresh strength.*
> *They spread their wings and soar like eagles,*
> *They run and don't get tired, they walk and don't lag behind.*
>
> Isaiah 40:31 (MSG)

> *There's an opportune time to do things, a right*
> *time for everything on the earth.*
>
> Ecclesiastes 3:1 (MSG)

> *Moral character makes for smooth traveling; an evil life is a hard life.*
> *Good character is the best insurance; crooks get trapped in their sinful lust.*
>
> Proverbs 11:5–6 (MSG)

ONE
FRIED ICE CREAM

I will wait
Until I see
The promise in your Word.
I will wait
Until I have
The promise of your Word.
I will wait.

HAVE YOU EVER tried it?

I couldn't quite wrap my mind around the recipe. How can you deep-fry frozen dessert? Ice cream will melt at the touch of an upward swing in temperature, so how does it retain its consistency in intense heat?

Out of curiosity, I ordered fried ice cream when I saw it on the menu. I was excited to try this fried treat. After a delicious scoop, or should I say bun, of ice cream, I requested for the recipe from the chef.

It's quite simple, really. The ice cream is spooned onto an already frozen tray and returned to the freezer. The batter is prepared: I think flour, breadcrumbs, eggs, and whatever else.

While the oil is heating up, each ice cream scoop is dipped in the batter very quickly then again returned to the freezer. Once the oil is piping hot, the ice cream buns are dropped in one after the other until the cooked batter is golden brown. This takes only a few seconds and voila! The fried ice cream is served. And you have to eat it very quickly.

Sometimes before God releases us to do anything worthwhile, He takes us on a journey far outside our comfort zones and puts us in the most bizarre situations, just as the ice cream is wrapped in batter.

He takes us back to our comfort zones for a season to heal. Then wham! He drops us in hot oil and we scream, "Get me out of here!" Before we know it, He lifts us out and places us in a waiting area, like the fried ice cream is placed on a kitchen towel to drain the excess oil, to drain us of every ounce of flesh.

At the time when we cannot glory in our flesh anymore, when we've been stripped of everything that represents our old nature, He presents us to a waiting public. Slowly they crack the outer shell, and all of our inward goodness oozes out to bless others. Welcome to the new you.

Do you have a vision of your future? Have discovered your purpose yet? Are you excited at what you and God are set to accomplish? Get ready for the hot oil. It will be intense, because the gold needs to be melted and molded into a similar image of God.

But remember, it's only for a season. Jesus endured the cross for the glory that was set before Him. So must we.

Let these verses reassure you: "Looking unto Jesus, the author and finisher of our faith, who for the joy that was set before Him endured the cross, despising the shame, and has sat down at the right hand of the throne of God" (Heb. 12:2 nkjv); "I wait for the Lord, my soul doth wait, and in his word do I hope" (Ps.130:5); and "But they that wait upon the Lord shall renew their strength; they shall mount up with wings as eagles; they shall run, and not be weary; and they shall walk, and not faint" (Isa. 40:31).

PONDER THIS:

Even when the heat of life appears to singe you, God will not let us handle more than what we can bear. He always delivers completely. Sometimes we have to wait for deliverance, but God never wastes any moment of our lives. Later, when you look back, you will see what God achieved in your life.

TWO
DON'T MESS WITH MY MIND

I have been told a lie
That God is not enough,
But often when I try,
Nothing else seems to satisfy.
But when I look into His Words,
My heart flutters with joy
At the name El-Shaddai,
The One who's more than enough.

IN THE EARLY seventies, and perhaps up till the late eighties, it was common practice in Africa not to eat at your neighbor's house, you know, in case they sprinkle some deadly stuff on the food.

The practice was to politely decline the meal and just pretend to enjoy the company.

Well, as a child I loved food. I wasn't allergic to anything edible. If it looked good and smelled good, it went straight into my mouth.

One day Mum, Sister, and I went for a walk in the neighborhood and stopped by a family friend's house. Right from the staircase the whiff of cooked beans assaulted my nostrils. My tummy grumbled, and it didn't matter that we had eaten just before we left home. I had a superfast digestive system, and right about then I was ready for the next meal.

This kind woman ushered us into the sitting room and went back to the kitchen. Mum sat beside Sister while I took the only other available seat opposite them. As we watched the television, Mum's friend came back in carrying two plates of hot steamy, well-spiced beans. She offered them to Mum and Sister, but they declined. When she stood before me, I deliberately looked away from Mum, engaged our hostess's eyes, and smiled with delight.

It was customary that when we went out and were offered food, we had to look at Mum to learn if she approved our accepting it or not. If she approved, she'd give a slight nod. But more times than not, she didn't approve. She'd pinch us if we sat close, or she'd wink, give a dark look that indicated "Don't you dare touch that food." Sometimes she flashed a pleading look that said, "You don't know what they put inside." Her last resort was the threatening look that said, "Wait until we get home and you will see what I will do to you." You all know the parental threatening look, right?

But I loved food, and at that moment, the temptation was greater than my common sense or fear of reprimand. I smelled temptation, heard it being offered to me, and it looked good. My next step to seal the deal was to taste it. I can imagine the Devil painting grandiose pictures of the beans in my mind, telling me it's sweeter than what I had eaten at home, and that I would be missing out if I didn't taste it.

In fact, the Devil would make me act like I'd never eaten beans before in my life. All I needed to do to stop the downward spiral, to curb the pseudo-hunger, to arrest my longings was to look to Mum, but I ignored her winks and body language and took the food offered to me. I chose to look away from the daggers and missiles I knew were flying across the room at me, and I ate that food with relish. I enjoyed it and scraped the plate clean . . . but at a great cost.

Oh, let me spare you the details of what happened when we got home. Good ol' Robb, the ointment they stick in your bum to cause your tummy to tingle and empty its content, came in handy.

To resist the temptation even as the food was being offered, all I needed to do was to look into Mum's eyes and I wouldn't touch the food. She was conveying enough messages of love and warning to keep me from falling, but I was consumed by my fleshly longings.

All Peter needed to do was to keep his eyes on Jesus and he would completely walk on water. The moment he took his eyes off of Jesus, the "wind became boisterous." It's amazing how he didn't notice the wind until then.

That's the job of the Enemy, to steal our attention with fearful or tantalizing things; to give us an easy option. His plan is to kill, steal, and destroy, but he won't come with a placard revealing his true motives. He'll decorate sin and death as the most desirable thing. He'll wrestle for our attention, our focus, and get us into compromising situations. No wonder sexual temptation mostly comes wrapped in pleasurable people, situations, and things.

We need to keep our focus on Jesus if we would walk on water, if we would find the doorway out of a tempting situation, if we would win the war against our mind, our flesh, our faith, our finances, our health, or our well-being. The King of glory is the author and the finisher of our faith, and He is able to keep that which is committed into His hands. He is able to keep us.

When we keep our eyes on Him, we are able to remain focused and steadfast. Remember these verses to help you keep your eyes fixed on Jesus: "A faithful witness will not lie: but a false witness will utter lies" (Prov. 14:5); and "They that observe lying vanities forsake their own mercy" (Jonah 2:8).

Ponder This:

God often draws a line before we plunge into the depths of temptation. That line is His loving warning of what's to come. If we keep our eyes on Jesus, He will help us walk on air over and above the line.

THREE
GOD'S OXYMORON

God said the sun would shine
In the midst of an angry thunderstorm.
God said my hands would carry babies
From a dry and empty womb.
God said there's an overflow
When the desert sand slips through my fingers.
It is God's oxymoron, His specialty,
To call those things that be not as though they are.

IMAGINE YOU ARE all set in front of the white lines. Your sneakers are top-notch, with spikes, cushion springs, fluorescent green glow, and bearing the Nike logo. You're warmed up and ready. You flex toned muscles and feel them ripple. You've trained for months and years for this one moment of glory. You hear the cheering crowd and see the finish line only meters ahead of you. Just a quick burst and will make a new record. Your running mates are no match for the years of running up craggy mountains and down pebbly valleys, through muddy waters and thick bristly mangrove forests. You have raced against time itself. You've done it all and with the best speed ever. Now this race on smooth solid ground with enhancements is a piece of cake. You take in a deep breath and wait for the whistle to blow. In a few moments the race will be over. You imagine the medal, cradling the pure, solid gold disc while cheers of triumph thunder around you. This is a winner and that's for sure.

But wait!

The race starter holds up a yellow flag. He points at you and walks toward you. Your heart skips a beat and you wonder what you've done wrong. His looks are not menacing, yet you feel unsettled. You check yourself quickly to be sure everything is in order. Shoes and sports gear are the right type and fit. You stand perfectly behind the white line.

So now what?

He marches up to you and gives you the most bizarre instruction: You are to change direction. You are to run away from the finish line. How can you win the race if you miss the target? You give the race starter a questioning look, but he maintains a blank stare. Does he understand what his instructions mean? Does he even know running away from the finish line will cost you the race? Does he understand your years of training and all the hard work it has taken you to prepare for this moment in time? Does he understand you are ready, experienced, and able? Does he know this could possibly be your moment of glory? But most important, does he not want you to win the race?

Then the whistle blows!

Like a whoosh of wind, your running mates take off, and so do you but against the same wind that would have pushed you to the finish line.

Now let's flip the pages of the Bible to a familiar character. In walks a seasoned and faithful servant of God. He'd just had a startling revelation. The God of the universe had a tête-à-tête with Abram and took him out in the evening to count the stars, which, God said, would be fewer than the number of children the man would have. When the man counted to one million, he could no longer continue, his exhaustion overtaking him. Phew! Fancy that many children? Talk about an exploding imagination.

But really, all Abram wanted was just one child, one little teeny-weeny pitter-patter. But no, God had to whet his appetite. Scores and scores of children, priests, kings, soldiers, mighty men of valor, women of destinies, and so much more would call him father. Then God painted a more grandiose picture of exceeding great reward, God being his shield, and made many more promises.

"Okaaay, I get the picture," Abram responded. "But, Lord God, what will You give me, seeing I go childless, and the heir of my house is Eliezer of Damascus?" Then Abram said, "Look, You have given me no offspring; indeed one born in my house is my heir!" (Gen. 15:2 NKJV).

Wow! So he needs just one little person and God shows him a million and more little people, as well as other benefits. What an oxymoron!

Do you find the opposite happening to you, especially on the heels of a promise from God?

God opens your eyes to give you a glimpse of His wonderful plans for your life, and all you need to do with the keys He releases into your hands is simply to reach out and unlock the door. Then hell unleashes its fury, sending you hurtling in the opposite direction of God's desired plans for your life.

Does that change anything? No! Maybe the time of the expected acquisition of God's promise may falter, but definitely not the perfect timing for the release of the promise.

Who blows the whistle at the start and finish of any race? The starter. The starter knows the beginning, the duration, and end-point of the race.

In God's semantics, opposites work for our good. You see, the Author of Life is your starter and my starter. He is there at the beginning of the race, the entire duration of the huffing and puffing, and at the finish line when you burst through.

Jesus Christ, our Lord and Savior, the author and the finisher of our faith, determines the finish line—wherever he puts the red tape, that's where the finish line will be.

In God's race there are no losers. He is at the beginning of the race and at the end of it. He alone determines where and when you finish, if you commit to Him and allow Him to blow the whistle. The only qualification for winning is to hear God's whistle and run. It doesn't matter where people deem the finish line. Only one Person determines your finish line, even when it seems you're going contrary to everybody else's direction. Once you have your eyes on Him, you're right on course.

PONDER THIS:

Does it seem you're farther away from your destiny? Does it seem the very opposite of what God promised is happening to you? If God blew the whistle and you're running in the direction of His leading, rest assured that you will not only finish but you will finish well.

FOUR
GOOD PEOPLE ARE STILL IN THE LAND

Why am I so angry
And ego bruised
In the midst of many troubles
That I seek to handle
All on my own?
Could God be slow to rescue?
Should I help Him mete out justice
To all those who offend me?
Even when I ignore the truth,
That wisdom and anger
Cannot abide
In the same drum
That thumps God's praise.

TWENTY MINUTES INTO what I hoped would be an uneventful flight, the Boeing 747 remained at the start of the runway because of a medical emergency.

My daughter was restless. It had been a long day, lunch was hours away, airport security checks frazzled her, and reuniting with her dad was the number one priority on her mind.

She unfolded her tray and asked for rice, her new favorite food, especially with fried stew and chicken or meat. I felt sorry for her, knowing she wasn't going to get any rice on this flight. Five minutes before takeoff, the cabin crew waltzed down the aisle for last minute safety checks. I was all set and didn't envisage any problem.

Until my daughter, who had been quietly playing with her coloring book, refused to have her seat belt on. Then began her tirade and tears and acting out. She'd rejected her seat and scooted onto my lap. The confused flight attendant went back to the cabin for help. A male crew member brought some cookies and spoke softly to my daughter, trying to convince her to take her seat. She finally complied, and we breathed a sigh of relief as the plane started taxing.

Then things went horribly wrong.

She didn't just cry, she yelled the place down. She wiggled out of her chair to sit on my lap. I placed her back in her seat over and over again, trying to calm her down, but it only aggravated her. The only respite we got was when she got back on my lap.

Now imagine this: dim cabin lights, soundless space, and the plane speeding down the runway with a two-year-old screaming at the top of her lungs and with no seat belt around her. What would any mother think or do?

The panic I saw in her eyes prompted me to follow my instincts. At the risk of safety, I cuddled her to my chest and we held on tight as the plane lifted off. It was odd because she'd never had a panic attack, nor had she ever been averse to flying. Just then, the man in the front seat turned back and shouted, "Will you get that child to shut up and control herself! Is she the only child on this plane?"

I was too stupefied and shocked to make a comeback. Then the professor behind me added, "Will you control that child and get her to stop yelling."

By this time I was still trying to soothe my child and wrapping her in the safety of my arms. I was filled with mixed emotions: confusion at my daughter's panic and anger at the insensitive remarks from the two passengers.

I thought of ways to spit back at the man. I thought of clever words to pierce his conscience, bust his ego, diminish his manhood, and reduce his grey hairs to foolishness. But alas, I knew Whose I am: a woman who has chosen to do things God's way, even when it hurts. I shut up and said nothing.

When we reached cruising level and the lights came on, I noticed a white man on the opposite seat giving the man in front of me a disapproving look. My daughter slept the entire six-hour flight, thankfully, on her own seat. I was grateful to God for the rest and respite. At the end of our journey, another white man behind me, whom I hadn't noticed before, came and asked if my daughter was okay. I nodded. He said he thought she was panicky, nervous, or simply tired. I nodded again, as I had no better explanation to offer but was grateful he inquired. Another young Nigerian guy came over and asked about my daughter.

When we got to our destination, it warmed my heart when the cabin crew came over to find out how she was doing.

Just at the moment when I sort of gave up on humanity, when I erroneously thought those two men represented all people, God brought six others to prove and show that I shouldn't lose faith in people.

There's always hope, and good people are still in the land. "The discretion of a man deferreth his anger; and it is his glory to pass over a transgression" (Prov. 19:11). "The Lord is merciful and gracious, slow to anger, and plenteous in mercy" (Ps. 103:8).

PONDER THIS:

People can be either pawns in the hands of the Devil or vessels in the hands of God. Having this perspective helps cut us some slack. We don't need to be all wound up and easily offended by people. Offenses will definitely come, but don't let them build a castle in your life.

FIVE
RESTORATION RIGHTS

Return and rebuild me, O Lord,
For I surely need that you restore all
That I thought I had,
Which I never had because I was lied to.
Restore the truth, O Lord,
As I ponder Your Words
That I may fully grasp all
That is truly mine.

SEVERAL YEARS AGO, for the most unearthly reason and according to unreliable local sources, the Kainji Dam (our national electric generating dam) refused to generate enough electricity, even though it rained cats and camels every other day. So typical of electricity in Nigeria, or we were being lied to.

I imagined the rain clouds avoiding the dam the entire rainy season and yet dumping its fill on the rest of the country in an attempt to cooperate with those enriched by power outage. But that's not even geographically possible, because God rains on both the just and unjust, including the dam and those perpetrating evil by ensuring we all spend our hard-earned cash on electric generators, petrol, and diesel; and, of course, not counting the noise pollution and danger.

Well, summarily we got used to unceasing power outages. We learned never to question the authority, and to consider it normal to live on candles, lanterns, and generators. In fact, having a power generating set is seen as affluence.

When the stress was too much to bear, Hubby and I took a short holiday to the United Kingdom for a much deserved rest. Because we had been conditioned to the maladies of our country, including seeing electricity as precious as gold, I made sure I ironed all my clothes before retiring for the night—you know, in case Nepa (as we call the fountain of electricity in Nigeria) strikes.

Now this thoroughly amazed our hosts, as they wondered at the feverish way I worked to iron out the wrinkles, as though I was in a competition. I explained my purpose, and they reminded me that Nepa hadn't and would never be granted a visa to the United Kingdom, not even for a short stopover.

Phew! Amidst the hilarity of the situation, I sighed deeply, knowing I had left Nepa behind.

But one cold evening as we took a stroll down the road, well wrapped up and enjoying the clean fresh air, we stopped at a corner shop to pick up some groceries.

Just as we walked along the aisle, tossing items into the shopping basket, the overhead lights blinked. In a flash, the store plunged into pitch-darkness. Lights were out not just in the store but also at every building down the street. The emergency lanterns came on and cast dim shadows everywhere.

And guess what my first exclamation was? "Oh shoot, Nepaaaa." Then I hissed.

The shop clerk gave me a rather curious stare, cocking his head. I guess he must have thought I was cussing in my language. It did occur to me that this was the United Kingdom, and a power outage should be a strange thing, but I felt that familiar crippling, depressing feeling when Nepa struck.

I was thinking of the dark and the smell of burned candles and acrid smoke curling up from the generator. I snapped out of it when trucks rumbled down the street, carrying mobile transformers and hooked them up.

The lights blinked and full power came back on. I shouted, "Uuupppp, Nepaaaaaa!"

The store clerk and some shoppers clapped at my outburst of victory, or should I say, "language interference excited exclamations." They didn't know what I said or what it meant, but they shared in my exuberance. Hubby had the good sense to nudge me and remind me that we were not in Nigeria.

It's not peculiar to me. Trust me, when you're a Nigerian abroad and there's a power outage, the first thing that comes to mind is *Nepa*.

I was amazed at the swift actions taken by the power company to restore power. It was the right of the citizens to have electric power, and the government ensured it was restored in record time.

The citizens expected it. But there I was shouting and rejoicing over something we were supposed to have full rights to in Nigeria. We pay our taxes and bills promptly, yet we still don't get electricity. When we do, if only for a few seconds, we celebrate and rejoice. No wonder Nepa is still the most famous tyrant in Nigeria.

May we never settle for anything less than God's best. Amen.

Imagine God owning the whole universe and the Devil offering Jesus a few kingdoms of the world just so Jesus could bow down and worship him (see Luke 4:5). It's like offering a teaspoon of water to quench our thirst for a price and denying us access to a gallon of water in our own backyards.

Imagine again, God our Father owns the whole universe and the Devil offers us a tiny plot with the effrontery to add a price tag to our own property.

May we not be deceived and ensnared by the tricks of the Devil. Everything the Enemy has stolen in our lives will be restored in full. *Everything*. (See Joel 2:23–27.)

This year, for your shame you will receive double and the Lord will embarrass you with His blessings. You will overcome, pursue, overtake and recover *all*. No good thing will He withhold from you in Jesus's name. "And I will restore to you the years that the locust hath eaten, the cankerworm, and the caterpillar, and the palmerworm, my great army which I sent among you" (Joel 2:25). "And he shall be unto thee a restorer of thy life, and a nourisher of thine old age" (Ruth 4:15a).

PONDER THIS:

When God restores, it's often with mega added benefit. Very comforting when you've lost a lot, isn't it? Just like the seasons, there's a time for restoration. Wait for it!

SIX
DO YOU DECAF?

My flesh whispered
Let's go over there
And have a day filled with pleasures
My heart is faint within me
As it tugs me away
My mind says, it's only for a short while
After all, we're not swallowing the whole lie
It reasons just before bait and snare looms
Right to the core of my heart.

ONE CUP OF delicious freshly brewed coffee tantalizes the taste buds and gives a shot of needed adrenaline . . . until the medical journals warn of an overload of caffeine in the blood. The producers, manufacturers, and marketers came up with an alternative called decaffeinated coffee.

Coffee drinkers who would normally consume maybe four cups a day might increase their intake, say, up to six or more cups when they switch to decaf.

The truth is that switching to decaf and increasing the number of cups consumed does not preclude one from the damaging effects of caffeine. In fact, decaf coffee comes with its own baggage, like acid erosion, cholesterol, heart attack risk, osteoporosis, rheumatoid arthritis, glaucoma, cancer, and organ damage. (You'll find a full report on decaf coffee on www.steadyhealth.com.)

For someone who loves coffee, switching to decaffeinated was quite a challenge. I enjoy the aroma, the velvety dark, wicked taste, and the euphoric effect caffeinated coffee gave me. I favored coffee sweets when I'd reached my daily limit of coffee, because the withdrawal symptoms were unpleasant.

Changing from full-bodied caffeinated coffee to decaffeinated didn't solve the problem. In fact, it gave me the latitude to increase my intake, which only made matters worse. But one day, I quit—just like that. No drama or fireworks. I just quit treating coffee like my life depended on it. I no longer saw it as a "must have" but a "could have."

It's pretty much like when people who are slaves to addictive habits desire to quit, but the advertisements and marketing companies come up with a new name for the same thing. They tell you it is less addictive, does less obvious damage, or is a lesser evil. The twenty-first-century hype gives room for indulgences cloaked by the latest ideas or ideals. So the advertisers play with our wit, and so not to appear extreme, they offer us a middle point, a subdued version of something that would naturally repel us. Sometimes it goes by the name "alternative lifestyle," or sometimes it's called the latest upgrade, latest thinking, and so many other pseudonyms. The idea is to get us to accept questionable lifestyles.

But here are a couple of verses that have haunted me recently: "Abstain from all appearance of evil" (1 Thess. 5:22); "Abstain from evil [shrink from it and keep aloof from it] in whatever form or whatever kind it may be" (AMP).

The bottom line for believers is not to be fooled by hype. We don't test the strength of our character by yielding to sin; we test it by abstaining from it, even when the lure is greatest.

The Bible cautions us to abstain from the likeness of anything sinful. It's like coffee. Coffee is coffee, decaf or not. One's effect is obvious, the other less obvious, but both have basically the same short- or long-term effect.

There's no lesser or greater sin. Sin is sin is sin. That's the neat, pure, unadulterated truth. Once your conscience is tugged, your purity is compromised, your devotion to God is questioned, there's no scriptural justifiable end; there's obviously something wrong and our internal alert should start to beep. We can't replace sin with a supposedly less obvious sin. But we can shirk its hold on us and hang on to the anchor of our souls: Jesus.

Ponder This:

Edward T. Welch put it well in his book *Blame It on the Brain?: Distinguishing Chemical Imbalances, Brain Disorders and Disobedience*: "The Bible has a different view of how we first get involved in addictions. Instead of explaining the overpowering urge for [something] as a disease, the Bible talks about our motivations and desires, forces so powerful that they can take over our lives. The Bible says that we first choose our addictions, and only then do our addictions choose us."

SEVEN
E NOT YOUR OWN, E MY OWN

The whole world is mine,
Even the trees and sky are mine,
Till He shows me the glory of the world.
You want it? He asks.
Bow to me and I give it to you.

"E NOT YOU OWN, e my own" my daughter says whenever I get her a new toy or plaything. She gets possessive to the point where it seems the gift originated from her, not me. In fact, sometimes she goes as far as hiding the toy to make sure nobody, including me, has access to it. She often reminds me, "E not your own, e my own," to which I usually nod then explain to her the need to share.

Yes, she says the initial thank-you, but that's it. From then on, I have no other rights. And I'm fine with that, but I do have rules for the use of "her gifts," one of which is that she can't take them with her to school. She fights me on this point, but most times I can make her see the sense in leaving them behind.

Other times I fail woefully and have to pacify her at the end of the day when her toy is either missing in school or smashed. But when I get a chance to recover, repair, or replace it, she quickly reminds me, "Mummy, e not your own, e my own."

I believe we do that with God at one time or another. We regale His gifts more than Him. We forget He is the originator of everything we own. He blesses us with life and other good things, and then we quickly ascertain that it's *our* lives and we can do whatever we want with them, thus sometimes living contrary to His original purpose and design.

He solicits our audience and courts our consent. He even left heaven to become like us, just to save us from destruction. Yet we dare place expectations on how He can meet our criteria of what, when, and how to believe, because we proclaim regarding our lives, "E not your own, e my own."

We either bury His gifts and talents, waiting for a platform, pulpit, or big break; or use His gifts and talents to serve the Enemy. When He gives us rules about using His gifts, we question His authority. After all, "E not your own, e my own."

Some go as far as questioning His existence by asking, "Who did you say you are again?"

I have had to pause and ask myself over and over again, Whose am I? Who runs the affairs of my life? Whose gift of life, talents, and abilities do I claim to possess?

Do I give the author of my life free rein to direct the use of His blessings, appreciate Him for His gifts by using them for His glory, or do I say, "E not your own, e my own?"

Selah!

Ponder This:

Can we sigh . . . deeply? Looking at things from God's perspective puts things into proper perspective. So let's sigh and let God.

EIGHT
WASTED SPACES

Fill every corner of my thoughts
With your thoughts, O Lord.
Fill every corner of my life
With your purpose, O Lord.
That my life might count
For beauty and purpose.

I ENJOY HOUSE WATCHING. I have a thing for architectural masterpieces, the kind of design that makes you dream of owning your own.

When viewing some of these homes, I wonder how much effort—time, money, and energy—went into the design, the survey, the materials, and the construction.

However, badly constructed houses stop me in my tracks. I once saw a house with a little landing on the outside, which I assumed was a veranda, but it had neither windows nor access door. It looked like an extension without any purpose. It led me to assume three things:

1. It was part of the original design of the house, but somewhere along the line, the design was either modified due to inadequate funds or simply the veranda didn't fit into the new design.

2. The design was intact, but at the last minute the builders or owners

decided they had no use for the veranda, by which time it was too late to reconstruct it.

3. They hoped to do something with the space but discovered it wasn't the most practical thing.

Some architectural designs are like wasted spaces. They look good but serve no purpose.

I would hate my life as a believer to be meaningless, a waste of space. Every experience we have, every adversity we face, every person we connect with, and every encounter in our lives are for a purpose.

There are no coincidences or sheer luck in the life of a believer. Our lives have been carefully marked and planned for a divine purpose. When we go through adversity, we wonder if it was really necessary. But I know if it wouldn't serve a purpose, God wouldn't let us go through it.

A biblical example is John the Baptist. The issue was not how old his parents were but what time he needed to be born. It wasn't a coincidence he was born six months before our Savior. John had a divine purpose: to be "the voice," the one who heralds the coming of the Messiah. That was his purpose.

God has a purpose for each and every one of us, and the onus is on us to discover it. We're not here to simply occupy space and time. We have been created for a purpose.

What's your purpose? Discover it, learn it, pursue it, and fulfill it. You and I are not wasted spaces. We will occupy till Jesus comes. Amen!

Ponder This:

Don't for one second waste everything God has put inside of you. Don't participate in activities for no reason or because others are doing it. Live life with a purpose in mind. That's what God created us for: purpose. Pursue yours and don't let it go to waste.

NINE
ONE HUNDRED KM/H

I am better than you,
Only where I function best.
You are better than me,
Only where you function best.
We are just the same,
Where God functions best,
His love to us, that is.

THE METALLIC BLUE car sped down the untarred road, churning up puffs of dust. It screeching as it veered left onto the asphalt road heading downtown.

"Take it easy, dear." She gripped the black leather seat as her feet pumped an invisible brake pedal, fear forming a lump in her throat.

He glanced sideways at her but said nothing. He reached for the dashboard, slotted in a CD while negotiating a bend with the fluid movement of a seasoned driver.

"Oh my God!" she yelled. "You almost cleared that yam seller." She checked the side mirror, expecting to see an angry, fearful woman yelling expletives, but the yam seller appeared oblivious to the passing cars, least of all theirs.

"Why are you taking this road?" She took in the unfamiliar territory, her eyebrows knitted in a frown. "Why can't we take the expressway?"

He rolled his eyes and let out a sigh.

"You see now, we're going to be late." She hunched her shoulders and checked her wristwatch. "Are there no other shortcuts?"

"This is the best route to get there," he said.

"Anyway, you're going too fast." She leaned over to his side a little. "I can read the speedometer from where I'm seating. You're doing eighty kilometers per hour."

"So?"

"That's too fast."

"In whose books?"

She hissed. "Well . . . in mine."

He sighed again, grabbed her hand, and pumped it a couple of times for assurance. "Don't worry about it, okay? I'm being careful." He turned and winked at her.

"Okay, just don't go too fast."

They continued their journey in silence. Between eyeing the speedometer, checking her wristwatch, and trying to relax, she noticed a busload of women ridiculously stacked with tubers of yam swerve into their lane. The car suddenly jerked sideways and threw her back against her seat.

"Take it easy, take it easy! Oh no, not too fast! You're going too fast!" She gripped the dashboard with one hand and the door handle with the other.

He ignored her, deftly maneuvered the car, and safely slipped into the fast lane, far away from the giddy bus.

She hissed. "That was way too fast now. What kind of driving is this?"

He shifted the gear from sport to regular, sped to a shoulder of the road, and parked the car. He switched off the engine and turned to her. He cocked his eyebrow as he dangled the keys. "Would you like to drive instead?"

"I just might."

He shrugged. "Suit yourself."

She snatched the keys and climbed into the driver's seat. She gripped the steering wheel, adjusted her seat, and checked the rearview and side mirrors. As soon as he was settled in, she shifted the automatic gear to drive, released the hand brake, and turned the car back on the highway. Feeling in total control and a rush of adrenaline coursing through her, she depressed the accelerator, oblivious of the speedometer's slowly climbing needle.

The cars on her lane dragged themselves. Feeling hedged in, she switched lanes, negotiated a free one, overtook a lone bus, depressed the accelerator further to overtake another car, and ate up the road, leaving the rest of the cars miles behind.

"At the rate you're going, you might miss the turn," he said.

She ignored him, turned the music up loud, and moved the car into the fast lane.

Sighting the sign turn right to Ikoyi too late, she slammed on the brakes, swerved sharply to the right and back to the left to avoid an oncoming car in the middle lane. She watched with horror at the speeding truck in the rearview mirror heading toward them.

"Move, move!" He screamed. "Step on it!"

She nodded and stepped on the accelerator, her hands shaking on the steering wheel, immobilized by fear.

He reached over and grabbed the steering, turning the car sharply away from the oncoming vehicle toward the service lane. In a second, the truck whizzed past, a rush of air rocking the car. She slammed on the brakes, pulled the hand brake, and rested back on the seat with a loud sigh.

He looked at her. "Are you all right?"

Unable to respond, she shook her head. Tears slid down her face.

He touched her shoulder and gave it a gentle squeeze. "Would you like me to take over?"

She nodded and slipped back into the passenger's seat.

He rested his hands on the steering and sighed. "You know . . . you were doing a hundred and twenty. That was way too fast."

He started the car and smoothly negotiated back onto the highway.

She knew. She let the tears tumble free. She understood how she'd judged herself better than this man. She understood the consequence of her actions.

* * *

Most times in life we deem ourselves better in some ways than others. In fact, we easily slander, judge, correct, and criticize others. "You can see the speck of dust in your friend's eye, but you don't notice the log in your own eye" (Matt. 7:3 Paraphrase mine). Can you imagine how ridiculous this is!

The sheer size of an iroko tree lodged in one's eyes is unthinkable (talk about major cataract surgery required). Yet someone whose vision is this severely impaired could strain to see the speck of dust in another person's eye. How utterly ludicrous is that? But that's how God views our judgmental attitudes. It can't be any clearer than this.

Do you find yourself itching to put others in their place, correct them, and rewrite their stories? Before you do, look first at your own shortcomings. Only then should you look at theirs with the eyes of compassion and understanding.

Consider this scripture: "If You, Lord, should keep account of and treat [us according to our] sins, O Lord, who could stand?" (Ps. 130:3 AMP).

Clearly, we are all fraught with faults and frailties. But God, who is compassion personified, overlooks our faults and loves us unconditionally. God expects us to be like Him. We're not there yet, but we can learn each day as we take one step at a time to give each person a longer leash than yesterday.

Remember:

> For the rest, brethren, whatever is true, whatever is worthy of reverence and is honorable and seemly, whatever is just, whatever is pure, whatever is lovely and lovable, whatever is kind and winsome and gracious, if there is any virtue and excellence, if there is anything worthy of praise, think on and weigh and take account of these things [fix your minds on them]. (Phil. 4:8 AMP)

PONDER THIS:

Come on, you know you're not better than your neighbors Mary or Harry. We may sin differently, but it's still all sin. And we may do things differently, and that's okay by God's law. We're different and that is very okay.

TEN
DETOXIFY ME, PUHLEEZE

Cleanse me
Of every guilt and filth.
Cleanse me
Of fleshly gratification.
Cleanse me
Of everything that gives me the right
Not to need you, O Lord.

SOME YEARS AGO, I decided to do a nine-day detoxifying fast. The idea for the first two days was to replace food with water—basically subsist on water and health juices—then gradually incorporate light meals for the remaining seven days. Sometimes just cutting down on food and eating only fruits, vegetables and drinking only water isn't enough to cleanse the body.

The first time I started this program and read the package details, I couldn't hide the smirk on my face. *Nine days. That's all?* I was confident this would be easy.

I woke up the next morning at 6 a.m., ready for my program. I psyched myself up and went for my usual brisk early morning walk, showered, prepared breakfast for the household, and prepared to ship toxins out of my life.

Oh, I had a swell time, really. To pump up my confidence, I immersed myself in reading up on all the health benefits of detoxifying. I weighed myself, measured my waistline, and entered all the necessary details in my workbook. On days three, six, and nine I would take the same measurements and record them.

By lunchtime my mind was playing tricks on me. I had only skipped breakfast and I was having that numb episode where nothing else made sense except the message my body sent to my brain and back to my body: Feed her . . . quickly!

My mind and body entered a tug-of-war: headaches, lethargy, drooling, and salivating at every smell coming from the direction of the kitchen. I grabbed my workbook, seeking reassurance.

The book stated that I would have headaches and might feel lethargic. It provided suggestions on ways to combat it: Get busy walking or doing something physically challenging.

That meant distracting myself and doing something constructive and engaging rather than sitting around on the pretext of watching my body rid itself of toxins. I had set the ball rolling, so I needed to get on with the program. But my stomach growled and, like a spoilt child, demanded food.

By sheer grace (at this point mere willpower did not do the trick) I marked the first day done. I went to bed smiling at my accomplishment. The next day, I literally dragged myself out of bed. I had little or no energy . . . no, scratch that, I had no gusto to face a foodless day. My mouth was dry and tasted like tar. My eyes drooped and I had no sugar left in my blood. Okay, I was done with this program, done and getting my groove back, I mused.

As I prepared school meals for my daughter and sandwiches for the man of the manor, I had the most philosophical questions run through my mind: Why on earth should/must we cut down or do without good food?

At what point did food become bad? Then this scripture came to mind: "And the earth brought forth grass, and herb yielding seed after his kind, and the tree yielding fruit, whose seed was in itself, after his kind: and God saw that it was good" (Gen. 1:12).

Everything God created was good, especially in its raw state. In the frenzy of modernization, we have created so many variations of food that we get only a small percentage of nutrients in each meal. There is, of course, junk food, which we desire and consume too much of, giving free radicals a good run in our systems.

Bearing in mind my goals and the immediate benefits I had already observed about the detoxify plan, I jettisoned the idea to reach into the fridge and pop something delicious into my mouth. Everything looked good, including the foil wrapping for the sandwich I was making!

Let's just say I did a waltz with the clock. It wasn't "hickory dickory clock." It was more like "It's gonna be over soon." And my mind and body screamed a staccato.

The greatest challenge for me was not just doing without food but preparing it, touching it, smelling it, while not being able to eat it. I was okay if I wasn't around food. I could think on other things.

A couple days into the fast, I fried some chicken and a little piece dropped on the plate, you know the bite-size you can quickly pop into your mouth as reward for service. Oh boy, was I so tempted! It was just a little piece, after all, and I figured it wouldn't mar the program. I picked up the chicken bit, fingered it, and gazed longingly at it, much like a starving urchin.

This wasn't written in the manual, this longing, wanting, desiring, and almost going nuts over a tiny piece of chicken. This itsy bit of chicken, a dead one, for that matter, was going to bring me down? Turn me into a deal breaker?

Well, thank God for grace, because somehow I managed to put it back on the pile as I finished my chore and left the kitchen.

On day three, I woke up and checked my measurements again. In two days I had shed a lot of water weight. In just two days. Understand that it's not the weight per se, but the elimination of toxic waste like excess salt and water. The detoxify diet opened my pores and made me sweat excessively. I had to consume more water than I normally would, and that in itself was mega healthy.

How many times have we had an urge to get rid of toxic thoughts? Everything we are, say, or do starts from our minds. As a man thinks in his heart (mind) so he is. You are basically the sum total of what you think about. You cannot live above your thought pattern. You reproduce what you ingest and digest. "Be not deceived; God is not mocked: for whatsoever a man soweth, that shall he also reap" (Gal. 6:7).

Each time I look in the mirror and see flab where it shouldn't be or a curve when there's no need for one, I get bothered about the additional weight, because I know it's nothing but saturated fat. And we all know saturated fat is no good for the body. We don't need it.

As Christians we have to deal with character flaws, sinful habits, and addictions that make us look less like our Savior. These habits and addictions are not only toxic to our bodies but also to our souls. There are times we need to detoxify our souls. We can opt for a full detox; replacing food with prayer and the Word, or we can do a partial detox of feasting more on God's Word. As children of God we have many ways to deal with those toxic wastes in our systems.

Initially, you may be all for a detoxification and jot down all your plans, goals, and aspirations, like reading the Bible every day. But once you start, expect your body and soul to rebel. Just as our bodies want food, it also wants comfort and latitude to do as it pleases. Consult the manual (the Bible) often for those times when you're severely tempted to give up.

Just like that piece of chicken, the smallest thing can cause us to fall, to compromise our stance. But the more we ingest and digest God's Word, the more the toxic habits are flushed out and replaced with a likeness of God. The toxic habits (character) gradually unsheathe the refined godly character growing on the inside. "But we all, with open face beholding as in a glass the glory of the Lord, are changed into the same image from glory to glory, even as by the Spirit of the Lord" (2 Cor. 3: 18).

Please remember that temptation is not a sin; it's yielding to it that leads to sin.

We will fall often, but getting up and trying again and again reckons us champions. We will be discouraged, irrational at times, yet retaining a tiny spark of hope on the inside counts. Knowing that life is not a hundred-meter dash but a marathon is all the push we need.

Get bothered by persistent sinful habits and get into the Word to detoxify your soul. God's Word has all the instructions you need to succeed. Leave the pupa stage behind, push and push, and get ready to fly. "Wherefore take unto you the whole amour of God, that ye may be able to withstand in the evil day, and having done all, to stand" (Eph. 6:13).

Ponder This:

Do you get tempted to do things you know you shouldn't? Temptation is often a sign that the Word of God doesn't have a firm hold in certain areas of our lives. It also indicates we're losing the battle of keeping our eyes on Jesus. That happens often, but God always makes a way out. There's a way out so we don't have to give in. Isn't that reassuring?

ELEVEN
YOU CAN TAME THE GROWL

Don't listen to the huff
Or the puff
Or the growl.
Animals need to exercise
Their vocals
Every now and then.

WE STROLLED DOWN the paved road, the evening sun behind us, when a young man with a ferocious-looking dog on a leash walked toward us. My daughter loves dogs, especially the docile one she often plays with at her grandmother's place. From the look on her face, I could tell she would love to play with this one.

As the man got closer, the dog barked and tugged on his leash. I walked quietly behind my daughter and her nanny, observing the dog's every move and the young man more, to be sure he had a good grip on the leash. We had almost gone past when the dog growled. Nanny did the most expected and heartbreaking thing. Overwhelmed with fear, she grabbed my daughter and made a mad dash for nowhere.

I expected the next thing that followed. The dog bounded after them while the young man desperately tried to restrain him with the leash. Though my heart flipped-flopped, I did the most sensible thing I could do at the moment. With no other choice but to trust the man and his leash, I spoke sternly to Nanny and ordered her to stop running.

She took one look at me as though I had utterly gone mad. I could imagine her reasoning, wondering how I could ask her to stop running when I should either be running too or screaming for help. She didn't stop but instead broke into a fast walk, clutching my daughter in her arms. My daughter wasn't happy and wriggled to be free so she could play with the dog. I caught up with them and she finally stopped.

By this time the dog had calmed a bit. He approached Nanny and sniffed around her. Sensing her fear he growled. Nothing to give him a good chase, he eventually became bored, quit resisting the leash, and walked away.

Nanny trembled with fear. If she hadn't been holding my daughter, I was quite certain she wouldn't have heeded my instruction. After the dog left, she gave me a questioning look. I took my time to explain my actions.

Generally, animals don't go looking for trouble. Dogs don't bite arbitrarily, but only when we give them a reason. Dogs love to run, so when you run, they take it as an invitation to play—they chase after you. Like most animals, dogs can smell fear when they come close and sniff you.

Because I'd had several dogs, I understood their character. It was natural for me to be proactive. If Nanny ran with my daughter in tow, the dog would chase after them. Being overwhelmed with fear, Nanny most likely would drop my daughter, fall down, run across the road, and still have the dog bite her or even both of them. I knew if I showed any emotion other than calmness, the dog would pick up the excitement in my voice and respond accordingly.

Just like a dog, the Devil can smell fear. Fear paralyzes and can send us hurtling down the road in insane directions. Fear can make you believe the Devil is bigger and stronger than God. It's amazing how, because of the potency of fear, so many promises in the Bible start with "Fear not."

God watches as the Devil comes close to you and sniffs around you searching for fear, searching to know if you trust God less, searching for readiness to throw down God's Word and make a dash for perceived safety.

Once he senses you're in fear, he growls just like a dog, to further confirm what he perceives.

The Devil is afraid of us, afraid of our taking God at His Word, afraid of what we can do with God's Word. He threatens us because he's afraid of us. Guess what? If you respond to his growling by running, you're heading away from true safety and right where he wants you: far away from God's safety net and protection.

The Devil growls and barks, threatening to lure you down the dark alley. The Devil cannot put you where you don't want to be, but it's important to know God's Word and understand how the Devil operates, as well.

But the Lord says to fear not. His angel watches over you. He that keeps Israel, neither slumbers nor sleeps. Fear not, dear child. (See Psalm 121:4.)

Ponder This:

Fear stinks. Faith breathes a heavenly fragrance. Which one would rather be wearing: the stink or the fragrance?

TWELVE
I MUST RESTOCK QUICKLY

Grace is like
My hair, my skin,
My food, my drink,
My present, my future,
And everything I am,
The very breath I take.

GRACE...

I cannot fathom its intricacies with my finite mind, yet I wholeheartedly embrace it, because without God's grace, I refuse to contemplate where I would be.

It will take eternity to fully comprehend it, and that's fine by me. I definitely want to spend eternity in awe of God's grace. Grace has a price, even when it seems free for me. All I can do is receive it. I can't work it out or pay for it. Jesus already did when He agonized at Calvary, His mind filled with thoughts of you and me.

But there's something else we are supposed to do with grace. Apart from receiving and being grateful, we're also expected to give it to others. We pay a somewhat similar price when we extend it to others. This is what I mean: "Therefore I take pleasure in infirmities, in reproaches, in necessities, in persecutions, in distresses for Christ's sake: for when I am weak, then am I strong" (2 Cor. 12:10).

Do you take pleasure in infirmities inflicted by others for the sake of Christ? Do you take pleasure in reproaches? Taunting and jeers? Dislike and disdain for the sake of Christ? Pleasure the same way you perhaps like ice cream, chocolate, or whatever strikes your fancy? Has this thinking ever crossed your mind?

I'll be honest; I don't take pleasure in suffering, dislike, disdain, others hurting me—especially for no apparent reason. I don't take pleasure in repaying evil with good or the many things I have suffered in the hands of people or those who rejected my hand of friendship the moment they realize I am a Jesus fanatic.

Yet, whether I like it or not, I have endured infirmities for the sake of Christ, and most times when I come out of it, I wonder who went through it in the first place. Grace must've seen me through.

Pray for your enemies and those who despitefully use you. That's what the Bible says, doesn't it? Have you succeeded in doing that . . . regularly?

A danfo driver cuts you off in mid traffic, and rather than spew expletives, send up a prayer for his soul. People cheat you, slander you behind your back, and the list goes on. I'm getting to the nitty-gritty of my own personal challenges. Yet God desires we look daily in the mirror of His Word in order to be like Him. That's the only way to develop Christ-likeness.

We don't devour the Scriptures for the purpose of arguing with others, showing off the revelations we've received, and the like. The Word of God is primarily for us to cleanse, renew, rebuild, restore, and conform to the image of Jesus Christ, our Lord and Savior. Freely I was given, freely I ought to give. I should never take His grace for granted.

Basically, when I struggle with being Christ-like with others, when I struggle to comprehend practical, sacrificial love, my storeroom of God's Word is depleted, and I must restock quickly.

I woke up this morning and wondered why I had to be good to this particular person and if this person appreciates all I've done in the last twenty years or so. God branded the verse from 2 Corinthians 12:10 in my spirit.

Until I start to take pleasure in infirmities for the sake of Christ, I have barely scratched the surface of what it means to be like Jesus. I have only begun to perceive what grace truly means, and I scarcely understand Jesus's suffering on the cross for my own sins.

Grace is free for me, but someone paid the price. And the price I pay is nothing compared with the pleasures of eternity when He will say, "Well-done, thou good and faithful servant."

Ponder This:

Yes, it hurts when people hurt us. Perhaps we hurt others too? Maybe more than we realize? God wants us to give others a long leash, after all; we're also at the end of a leash that is eternally long.

THIRTEEN
NAÏVE

We hold the truth in trust,
Like an hourglass,
In our hands.
Until deceit like a gust
Shatters every grain of trust.

NAÏVE . . .

Yep, that just about describes me to a tee. I tend not to put two and two together too quickly when it comes to people's motives. I take people at their word. That's not a bad thing, but it's also not always a good thing. Trust almost always comes natural to me, until it is broken.

I will digress a bit. We Christ believers are good at creating a façade, which gives people the impression we're perfect—we are not real people with real problems. That's why I love Joyce Meyer. Her message is deep, realistic, and applicable to everyone.

When I got to know Salt (www.thesaltchronicles.com), I was amazed at what she wrote in her blog, available for the whole world to read. Her blog diary is a chronicle of her life, her weaknesses and strengths, her failings and successes. She relates how God told her to share it all. Sometimes when I read some entries, I cringe, and other times I gasp. I mean, she loves God, is super excited about her salvation, and yet fully understands that being human and real is a sure way to be an effective witness.

People in our world need God badly. They need to know that Jesus loves them, does not condemn them, but desperately wants to deliver them from sin and the clutches of the Enemy. As much as we are to be separate from the world, we cannot put up defenses that shut people out or make them feel heaven is unattainable.

The message of the kingdom of God is simply the good news.

My question for you today is this: If God were to inspire men to write an addendum to the Bible, starting from, say, a century after the book of Revelation, and it covers the church's activities from then through the revivalists and all the way to our modern social media times, and this Bible documents everything—features you and me and our exploits of faith—would you mind if your dirty linen is documented in a book that many generations will read about?

Ahem! Truth be told.

You would have no say in the matter. Did David? Or Samson? Or Abraham? No. (Hehehe, I snicker cynically.) Nothing is hidden from God. Never mind looking holier than thou.

What's going on inside of you—away from prying eyes and itching ears? You can keep us all out but you can't keep God out. So in "acting" pious you deceive no one.

I read Lee Grady's article in *Charisma Magazine*, "7 Ways to Prevent a Moral Failure." Numbers two and seven jumped out at me. Connections. Accountability. Fellowship.

The Bible says that one person can chase a thousand, but two people can more than quadruple that number. We must connect with one another. In connecting we must be real. And in being real, we must be able to trust one another. In doing so, we can safely be ourselves. Shouldn't we be safe with our brothers and sisters in Christ?

God knows how naïve I can be. I met Christ at the tail end of the Scripture Union era when the fear of God compelled us to be who we profess to be to people.

Nowadays, you can't know who's a "real" Christian but by the Spirit. If you spend time with them, then you can know by their fruits. For the very reason these issues are real and more so in the church, I suggest we prayerfully select people to befriend who are strong in faith, rich in God's grace, and full of God's wisdom—who are also very *real*.

Rarely am I close to anyone I cannot be real with and share my failings as well as share in theirs so we can prayerfully help each other (not counting mentors and parents in the Lord).

This Christian race is not to the swift or to the strong, but to those who endure till the end. Trust me, you cannot live a successful Christian life alone. You need the Holy Spirit and you need others too. So why do we pretend with one another? You must and should be connected with someone who is real and you can trust, steeped in the Word, and whom you can confide in and share your innermost thoughts. Nobody is perfect, so don't expect perfection, but, please, let's be real. We have an Enemy out there preying on our pretenses.

Until a weakness is confronted, it retains its grip over our lives. I don't condone taking God's grace for granted, neither do I lean toward excesses or overt worldliness, but let's help each other.

Be open and not judgmental. The church should be a place where we can get help in our weak areas. If you pretend you're super-strong, you set yourself up for an attack from the Enemy. Ask for help when you need it.

Yes, I have a problem. I am naïve. The same way I take God's Word without question is the same way I take people's words: without question. I am learning. It's strength in the sense that I don't often struggle with God's promises and instructions unless it involves sacrificing my Isaac. But then I would need a double dose of God's grace.

Naïvety is a weakness when I apply it to human beings. This is why the Lord said to be gentle as doves but wise as serpents; why God's church should be a safe haven. A place where you can tell me you'll pray for me and you really do, not because I will ask you the next day what God said to you when you prayed, but because you deeply care enough to petition God on my behalf. I want to be naïve enough not to be suspicious of you, but to trust that at least in your imperfections you are yielded enough for the Holy Spirit to work through.

I want to be naïve enough to believe strongly that when Jesus said He is coming back for a church without spot or wrinkle, He truly is, because

He will transform His church and the gates of the Enemy will be powerless against her.

Ponder This:

Can we be real for a change? Can we just splay the searchlight on the grey areas? At least can you be real with God? Tell Him as it is, warts and all. He can never betray you. Whom will He share your secrets with anyway?

FOURTEEN
WAVES AND WONDER

The wonders of the world
Never cease to amaze.
The glory of it all,
God made for you
And me.

GEOGRAPHY WAS MY best subject in school. I have no clue how it became so, seeing how much I love staying indoors and burying my head in books. Anyhow, I remember loving the drawings (I love to draw) and knowledge of the unknown. Something about physical geography is awe inspiring and spellbinds me: the splendor of the cosmos, the dunes, the stalagmites and stalactites, the folds, geysers, cascading waterfalls, and so much more. I cannot but be amazed at what I see.

Have you seen Niagara Falls or Victoria Falls? They are breathtaking. You just know this is one of God's handiwork, a little splash in His canvass of the world. It takes your appreciation of God up a notch.

We walked down the beach, Mum, Daughter, and I, picking up unusual-shaped pebbles and shells we would paint when we got back to our hotel room.

"Mummy, how come these rocks are round and smooth?" Daughter said.

I remembered geography class about rock formations. "Let's do a little geography, shall we?"

For thousands, even millions of years, little pieces of our earth have been eroded—broken down and worn away by wind and water. These little bits of our earth are washed downstream, where they settle to the bottom of the rivers, lakes, and oceans. Layer after layer of eroded earth is deposited on top of each. These layers are pressed down more and more through time, until the bottom layers slowly turn into rock.

Weathering causes rock to break into smaller particles. When these particles are transported by wind, water, or ice, the jagged edges from fractures are gradually worn down from abrasion with other particles, making the outer surface appear relatively smooth. Sometimes the mere abrasive effects of windblown particles on a rock will smooth the exposed surface, leaving the remainder of the rock jagged. Rounded and smoothed stones are the product of tumbling, which is usually accomplished by transportation of the stone by water and contact with other rocks.

The smooth stones we picked up had gone through a process to get from a little piece of dirt into the rounded smooth pieces we held in our hands. Lots of howling wind, freezing ice, splashing waves, and tumbling takes place before the finished product. Who would have thought mere constant contact with other rocks or splashing water can transform a piece of jagged rock?

Now take in a deep breath. Have you got that "aha" moment yet?

The continuous splashing water of the Word of God and constant contact with fellow believers will transform our lives? Yes, I got it too. It may take days, weeks, months, and even years, but like a gentle wave splashing against a cliff, eroding its sides to give it an eventual stunning shape, the Word of God will scour, erode, prime, and solidify us into God's image.

But it doesn't stop there.

That smoothed character comes from the constant grating and tumbling with others. The process is tedious. Years of daily study of the Word and its application to our lives will eventually produce a Christ-like image. But it takes time and patience.

At first it may seem nothing is happening on the outside, but just like the rock is formed from the depth of the ocean, so our characters are shaped from the inside out.

One of my devotional readings about character formation blew my mind. The writer said that the Holy Spirit worked on and formed Jesus's character, life, and ministry over thirty years. Every battle He would face in ministry was already won behind the scenes. When He fasted and the Devil tempted Him, He overcame, not at the point of temptation but way before, because He was steeped in the Word and therefore well grounded. So let the waves roll.

Ponder This:

The people who bump into our lives and make us "ouch" actually help fine-tune our characters. We become better persons as the days go by. That's why God lets them stay awhile, so that every rough edge is smoothened. We can look in the mirror of His Word and see more likeness of Christ daily in us.

FIFTEEN
SWITCH TO THE END

The end,
Is the beginning
From which God starts.
Heaven
Is the end
From which God begins.

I READ AN ARTICLE, "Top Tips for Plotting a Story," and it got me thinking.

When I read the first tip, Write the Ending First, I whooped. At first glance, writing the ending first doesn't make any sense. Why do that? It gives you a destination. When you know where you're going, it is easier to plot your journey. Hold a SatNav, flick it on, and the first thing it asks is your destination.

You have barely started the journey, but that gadget needs to know where you're heading. You punch in your ending address first, before you commence your journey.

In plotting my destiny, God started at the very end. You know, that place where it's all glorious and excitingly wonderful. Then He said: "Declaring the end from the beginning, and from ancient times the things that are not yet done, saying, My counsel shall stand, and I will do all my pleasure" (Isa. 46:10); and, "Before I formed thee in the belly I knew thee;

and before thou camest forth out of the womb I sanctified thee, and I ordained thee a prophet unto the nations" (Jer. 1:5).

This idea, this start at the end, is one of God's Oxymoron. I love it. We are not charting new courses. We are discovering our destinies. We are not only discovering our destinies, we are discovering the Master Plotter/Planner. In addition, we are now discovering how to work hand in hand with the Master to get us safely to that desired end.

Discover the Master

Discover Your Ending

Collaborate with the Master

Ha! Don't you just love sweet endings? And we will live happily ever after. Oh yes, that's a given.

Hey! Wait a minute. What about the "buts"? The grueling journey? The curveballs along the way? The pain and the losses?

Sometimes I sit down to think of how to measure eternity. I try to stretch my mind to a dangerous precipice. How do you measure eternity? We can't do it with our finite minds. We were not meant to. We were created to love, trust, and worship God. And time as we know it was created for us, for this side of heaven. So whatever happens within this fraction of eternity is only a fraction of eternity.

Back from my musing . . . I realize God never meant for us to go through anything alone. While the journey may sometimes be unpalatable, He promised He would never let us go through more than He has empowered us to bear.

It takes faith to draw on God's help when our world is rocked with adversity. It is tempting to think we can't go through certain trials without their crushing us, but the truth is that we are capable of much more than we think. Yes, we will feel pain just as we feel joy and pleasure, but even the joys of this world cannot be compared with eternity, when we will experience joy in an unprecedented way.

Since eternity is the beginning of the end of our now, let's switch to the end. It's much more fun.

PONDER THIS:

In switching to the end of our pain, we give ourselves room to believe again. Allow yourself to believe again in joy, in love, in God's goodness. Will you do that, please?

SIXTEEN
DANGEROUS MISSION

His words are dangerous,
Did you not know?
His words are powerful,
Have you not been told?
His words are sharper
Than a double-edged sword,
Clearer than the midday sun,
Like salve to a wound
And calm to a raging storm.

I'VE BEEN PARTICULARLY careful about too many things.

The Martha spirit has been running riot inside of me. Howbeit I cannot change anything, even myself, why worry about what I can't change? In spite of all the carefulness and self-proclaimed perfections, I still fall short. Trying to be perfect is a profession I have recently, specifically yesterday, written my letter of resignation to. I don't even want the gratuity.

I had the notion that I held the blueprint of my life firmly in my grasp, neatly tucked away to do with as I deem fit. Until I read that "Declaring the end from the beginning, and from ancient times the things that are not yet done, saying, My counsel shall stand, and I will do all my pleasure" (Isa. 46:10).

In other words, I have little or no say as far as my precious plans are concerned.

I wished I hadn't read that scripture. Once I had, I could not plead ignorance. And this scripture haunted me. It stripped bare the security in my cold calculated plans. Ouch! Following on its heels is the twin sister: "Behold, I have engraved, etched, imprinted (tattooed a picture of) you on the palm of each of My hands" (Isa. 49:16a AMP).

When you have no hiding place, you're in danger. You've lost control. The arsenal, the weapon, the sawed-off shotgun pointed at you is not only fully loaded, it is the Word. And the Word is: Quick, Alive, Active, Powerful, Operative, Effective, Energizing, Sharp; it Pierces, Penetrates, Divides, Discerns, Exposes, Sifts, Analyses, Judges motives, Discovers. (See Hebrews 4:12.)

You've been backed against a wall and blasted through and through. What do you do next? Surrender. Raise your hands in surrender. Praise Him like you just don't care that you've surrendered. You're past caring, anyway. You should be dead. A new being, a new life should have begun because: "I am crucified with Christ: nevertheless I live; yet not I, but Christ liveth in me: and the life which I now live in the flesh I live by the faith of the Son of God, who loved me, and gave himself for me" (Gal. 2:20).

Let me show you another dimension:

> Indeed, I have been crucified with Christ. My ego is no longer central. It is no longer important that I appear righteous before you or have your good opinion, and I am no longer driven to impress God. Christ lives in me. The life you see me living is not "mine," but it is lived by faith in the Son of God, who loved me and gave himself for me. I am not going to go back on that.
>
> (Gal. 2:20. MSG)

The Word is the perfect tool for conforming my life to perfection His way, not my ideas or theology. While I struggle to be perfect on the outside,

God desires perfection from within. Isn't that why I shiver when the Word pierces deep down?

It is a dangerous thing to study and live by the Word. You can't try to resurrect the old man, and you can't entertain Martha. (Sorry, Martha, you're a great woman of God. This is for illustration only.) You can't even flow with the stream of people. When the radar of God's Word zooms in on you and zips right through you, expect carcasses.

After the *logos* and the *rhema* of the Word of God have journeyed through your life, what's left of you, if anything at all, is what should be left.

It's a dangerous mission to study the Word, *n'est-ce pas?*

Ponder This:

I dare you to study the Word and see if you won't be blasted through with change. I dare you to study the Word and see if your world will not be turned right side up. I dare you to study the Word and see if you won't view life through rose-colored lenses. I dare you to study the Word and see if you won't see God.

SEVENTEEN
NUMBERS & STATS

Strands of our hairs
Are counted and treasured.
The number of our days
Are carefully measured.
The numbers are God's,
To show like the sun's rays,
His plans for our lives,
The rest of our days.

WHY ARE WE so obsessed with numbers?
I'm ranting again. *Pardon moi.*
I read a friend's Website article in which she wondered what we all really want when we start a writing Website and work toward gaining a thousand-plus followers. She said she wished she had that many followers, but then she questioned that at the end of the day, would that satisfy her? Would she feel complete, accomplished, loved, and famous? She answered with an emphatic *no*! Why did she feel at the end of it all she'd still not find satisfaction? Because she wanted to satisfy the audience of one, first and foremost. And that's God.

I'm not a mainstream writer. I'd like to consider myself primarily an inspirational writer or journalist. Sometimes I get all churchy and in that *rhema* mode, and I want to just unplug my mind. Though I don't do so often, I'd like to write about the mundane things that inspire me and bring me back into the worship zone.

Having said this, I don't write with a large audience in mind but to a target audience. Not everyone can be reached through the written word. Some people will not pick up a book, no matter how many miracle stories are stuffed in it. They're just not readers. Some prefer to receive knowledge and information through audio, visual (TV), or attending a live conference. And in my part of the world, not everyone gets online often.

So my target audience would be those who read and want to be inspired. I'm not pointing my arrow primarily at women, although I reckon I tend to pull in more women. I wish I could write about lifestyle, relationships, tips on "securing your marriage from infidelity," and other things people love to read. I can't. I'm not a novice, but I'm not inspired to write about issues of life. I simply love musing on mundane things in life that inspire.

But then I digress . . . as usual.

Salt (www.thesaltchronicles.com) concluded that she was happy writing what she loved to write and then allowing God to bring in those who need to read her articles. She wasn't saying that God will do any marketing or all the hocus-pocus thinking of us miracle-chasing Pentecostals. Absolutely nothing wrong with getting the word out about your book, writing, or vocation, but we must focus on the content. The question I ask myself is, what would God have me write about?

Is my writing true to who I am, and is it inspiring? Am I teaching someone something or stoking a dying ember in him or her or challenging my readers' mind-set or feeding them with much needed information? I tell you, sometimes when I read my own writing, I'm taken aback by what I've written. I don't mean to be pompous, but I get blessed again and again. And that's when I know I have been truly inspired to write.

I love that Buky (http://bukyojelabi.com/) prays over her writings before posting them online and then prays for the readers. It's focus. It's understanding what inspired writing as a Christian or an inspirational journalist like me is all about.

Let's get three examples of why the numbers of followers don't really matter. Why the stats don't have to be so high for you to feel you're making an impact or doing anything worthwhile. "And the Lord said unto Gideon, The people that are with thee are too many for me to give the Midianites into their hands, lest Israel vaunt themselves against me, saying, Mine own hand hath saved me" (Judg. 7:2).

Gideon had every intention of winning the war against the Midianites, and he had a good strategy—gather all able-bodied men together. But God saw two categories of people who shouldn't be there: the fearful and the unwise. For this particular war, He didn't need *everybody*. He needed just 300 men. A whooping 31,700 men went back home. God proved He didn't need to save by many. He didn't do the crowd thing.

Look at the two scriptures below and you'll see that, although we have a part to play, specifically that of planting and watering, God will draw the right people to you.

> And they, continuing daily with one accord in the temple, and breaking bread from house to house, did eat their meat with gladness and singleness of heart, Praising God, and having favor with all the people. And the Lord added to the church daily such as should be saved.
>
> (Acts 2:46–47)

> I have planted, Apollos watered; but God gave the increase. (1 Cor. 3:6)

So relax on the numbers game. Don't get all twisted when the stats don't go up, when your ministry doesn't double in number, when more people don't acknowledge your talent. Do what you can to get the word out. Pray for your readers, members, followers, and customers, and pray for God to draw whomever He deems would be blessed by your offerings. Leave the rest.

Like my mentor always reminds me: Ministry is not about numbers. It's about specifics, and if God sends you to only one person, do the job with all of your might. Always give it your best shot. That one person matters more to God than your trying to rake in a crowd.

PONDER THIS:

How would you feel if God zeroes in on you in the midst of a throng of people? Thrilled? Excited? That's how He wants us to treat people, with equal importance, not just part of a crowd.

EIGHTEEN
FOUNDATIONS

Foundations start
At the beginning of
God's promises.
Foundations end
When God turns
The wheels in motion.

THE OTHER THING about foundations is . . .

You have to dig deep if you want it to last long. And that's the invisible stage. The stage where the whole world wonders why you've got your head buried in the sand. While you're digging deep into the dirt, you must have a firm picture in mind of the structure you intend to build. In fact, that picture is what determines how deep you burrow.

Building a godly foundation requires first a birth. You have to be born into a family to grow and mature in that family.

The interesting difference between the physical family and the spiritual one is that the physical family tends to your growth to get you to the stage where you can start your own family. But in the spiritual, you're tended not to go off on tangent but to be fused together in a critically different capacity. The spiritual family is the body not factions, Christ is building. The body is the bride of Christ, and He is building and adorning His bride for Himself. We all are building to fit into Christ's image, because Christ, our groom, is preparing us for His second coming. He is concerned about whose image we are becoming. If we don't start to look like Him, He starts to chisel at our foundations, because something is clearly wrong.

Sometimes we build faulty foundations based on experiences, one bit of understanding or an aspect of life, or on general ideas and concepts. No other foundation is solid like the one built on the Word of God. We build mind-sets based on cultures, traditions, biases, and the like. Sometimes we don't even realize our beliefs are violently opposed to the truth. We may very often need a reengineering, a reorientation, or a recalibration to get us back on track where God wants us to be. I've had series of these in the past.

Early last year my foundation was yanked out from beneath me. I had become complacent with some things. I had lost the edge I required to be in top form. I was living on past revelations. God rattled my foundation by first recalibrating my mind. My old mind-set went first. Oh, I wept for the comfort I had known, though I was going nowhere with that mind-set. It's shameful when you discover you've been wrong all the while. It makes me cringe to think about it. Anyway, I badly needed the wake-up call.

It felt like I was starting all over again. You have the opportunity to see things from a different perspective, to see where and what you got wrong.

Nehemiah had to rebuild Jerusalem. Despite setbacks and the daunting tasks, he and his team succeeded. Moses had his foundation rebuilt in the wilderness; the children of Israel too had their mind-sets recalibrated. It's better to crumble when you're just starting out than to get to the decking and roof and then crumble. But if you do, just see it as an opportunity to get the foundation right.

Has it happened in your marriage when everything crumbled and you had to start again? Has it happened with your health? Your finances? Your almost everything? It's okay, even if it seems all hope is lost. There's always hope once we place our trust in God. "Therefore thus saith the Lord God, Behold, I lay in Zion for a foundation a stone, a tried stone, a precious corner stone, a sure foundation; he that believeth shall not make haste" (Isa. 28:16).

PONDER THIS:

A foundation built on Christ is the surest foundation there is. We'd best build on Him and His Word. Do you not agree?

NINETEEN
WHAT IF?

What if your life hovers
Between the present and the past?
What if your future
Is a slave to the present?
What if life
Leaves a trail behind
Of your dreams and your hopes?
What if God holds
A promise of the future
And hides it in your present?
What if God's Word,
Answers all your what ifs?
What then?

WHAT IF YOU could rewrite your future, what would you add? Would you change your folks, spouse, or children? Would you change your race or social status? Or maybe write all the fame, success, and riches into your future?

I read a novel about some books with mystical powers. Anyone who wrote in them could change the future. These books were well hidden, buried beneath an ancient monastery until four bright kids stumbled on them. Well, what do you know, they started to scribble on these books, and everything they wrote came to pass because the books had the ability to rewrite the future and erase the past.

These kids were brought up in an isolated monastery away from the evil and contamination of the world. Why the isolation? It was an experiment to see if evil could reside in the heart of a child untouched by the world. These pristine, supposedly innocent children got hold of the books, and through their writings and imaginations, they unleashed all the forces of hell. The question is, where did they learn evil if they had been sheltered from the evil of the world from birth? Or how did evil become entrenched in their hearts? That was the crucial question the novel set out to answer.

Back to my question.

What if you got a hold of such a book and you could chart your future; what would you write or wish for? Think about it.

How is this question related to the story above? Well, there's a fundamental problem with these kids. It has nothing to do with their sheltered lives or that they'd been innocent from birth. It has everything to do with their nature. They didn't need to be introduced to sin. Sin was their nature, the sin nature in an unregenerated person. "Lie not one to another, seeing that ye have put off the old man with his deeds; And have put on the new man, which is renewed in knowledge after the image of him that created him" (Col. 3:9–10).

Your nature will always catch up with who you are. You can tame and domesticate a lion all you like. But it can never be a pet; neither can you play with it with reckless abandon. It is inherently a wild animal and will remain so. Its nature may reside in dormancy, but give it room to self-express and you will see its nature unfurl in all its glory.

Again, permit me to ask: If you were given two empty journals to fill up to change the course of your life, one for your future and the other for your past, what would you write in them? What would you erase? What would you add?

Had I that choice, I would set aside the future and deal with the past book. No, I don't intend to erase all my past. I just need to change one thing. I need to move back a bit the day I shed the old sin nature, or better expressed: the day I assumed my originally God-intended nature—the day I met the Lord and I assumed my new nature, the day I plugged back into my true source. You see, that change of nature changes *everything*.

"I am crucified with Christ: nevertheless I live; yet not I, but Christ liveth in me: and the life which I now live in the flesh I live by the faith of the Son of God, who loved me, and gave himself for me" (Gal. 2:20); therefore, I needn't worry about the future, because in assuming the nature of my Father, the nature of dominion and glory, means I have a God-natured future in my grasp. Once I assume my God nature, everything else changes. If I merely changed my mistakes or my race or other things, I'd still arrive at the same place until I change my nature.

And I ask again: What if you had a dry erase board and a felt marker that can transform your past or future? What would you change?

Ponder This:

Change is constant, they say. So change is normal. The most significant change in our lives occurs in the heart. That's what can change ones destiny. Have you considered a change of heart lately?

TWENTY
BEAUTY AND GLORY

Though the sun blushes
In the eventide,
And the sky is sprinkled
With glittery stars,
Even the hush of waterfalls
And yawning petals,
The beauty and glory of it all,
Cannot compare
With God's beauty and splendor.

GOD BROUGHT SOMETHING to my notice and dangled it before my eyes so much that, even if I wanted to, I couldn't miss it: *words*.

I love words. I love words for their sake. I love what I can do with them. I love how words make me feel when they make people say "Hmmm" or "Wow." My love for words is all about me. I feel a kind of power in using words to stimulate other people's minds, to stir the heart, or even start a war. I just love words.

But lately I have begun to see as I delved into the Scriptures that, very simply put, God's words are weighty and not for show. Unlike ours, God's words are for the demonstration of power.

The essence of the Bible from Genesis to Revelation is to demonstrate who God is and what He is doing in the here and now, and to get a glimpse and a demonstration of the power of the ages to come. It's like a triangular affair: I get from God (power, dominion, authority), give to the environment (cultivate, subdue) to get back to me (fruitfulness, multiplication) in order to give back to God (glory, honor). Get it?

In Genesis, power was available to create, but no authority had yet been given until God spoke. He used words. In reading many instances of the spoken Word, I began to understand that just as the spoken Word is powerful, so is the written Word, the Bible.

I found myself oftentimes foraging into a glossary of words and, to borrow from Paul, "enticing words of human wisdom." If you know how to use words, whether in writing or in speech, you can be very persuasive, and, as I said earlier, you can start a war or broker peace.

Words are powerful and you can do so much more. I began to lean more to the words than their message. I wanted to always stun my readers. I wrote many engaging stories, and I was once labeled the "Queen of Shorts." I knew how to weave a whole book into a few lines and achieve the same satisfaction with all its intricacies.

When my cup was full, the inspiration to write dwindled. I struggled and clawed for inspiration and wrote poems on my missing muse, but nothing changed until I finally got it.

I wasn't meant to write for the sake of weaving words together to entice people with a gift that wasn't even mine to start with. I was meant, like the concentric triangle mentioned earlier, to give the glory back to God. The only way I could achieve that was to start with God. Get the blueprint and then move with a target audience in mind with the plan to give it all back to God.

Does it mean that because I was getting inspiration to write from God I should not be colorful in my writing? I should not show my peculiar flair or display my unique writing voice? Let me show you the answer in Exodus. "And take thou unto thee Aaron thy brother, and his sons with him, from among the children of Israel, that he may minister unto me in the priest's office, even Aaron, Nadab and Abihu, Eleazar and Ithamar,

Aaron's sons. And thou shalt make holy garments for Aaron thy brother for glory and for beauty" (28:1–2).

The books of Exodus and Leviticus have a laundry list of requirements for the priestly robe and attire. God was into specifics. He wanted the robes designed in a certain way. The purpose of the intricate design of the robes was for "glory and beauty." God didn't just want the priests to dress up according to what they desired. In representing God, He wanted them to look distinguished, excellent, and holy.

If you read the entire chapter, you'll be amazed at the details God gives for the robes.

God is as interested in what I write as how I write it. He didn't create clones, so He expects me to fully represent who I am in everything I do. And that means finding my voice, as we say in the writing world, or finding my niche and then producing the work. When I seek the purpose of my writing, I hope it's for both glory and beauty and not as Paul warned in 1 Corinthians 2:4: "And my speech and my preaching was not with enticing words of man's wisdom, but in demonstration of the Spirit and of power: That your faith should not stand in the wisdom of men, but in the power of God." The New International Version puts it this way: "My message and my preaching were not with wise and persuasive words, but with a demonstration of the Spirit's power, so that your faith might not rest on human wisdom, but on God's power."

If Paul's words and preaching were to entice with man's wisdom, it would be bereft of power and, therefore, would neither save nor deliver.

I have discovered that when we know who God made us to be and do, and we grasp our uniqueness, we can be true to our callings with no need to be manipulative.

Everyone has an audience, whether one or a zillion. Everyone has people who will read anything you write or listen to anything you say. While you're busy trying to be somebody other than who you were created to be and try to capture people who don't give a hoot who you are, you miss out on those people God has called to you. If we stick to who we are, our beauty—the beauty of what we do—will be evident to those God has called us to reach. And that saves us from leaning on man's wisdom.

Let me digress a bit.

Whatever God calls us to do, whatever our vocations as heaven's representatives, we must do it excellently (beauty) and with a view to giving honor back to God (glory.) We cannot do things any which way or for its sake alone, secular or not. In fact, we cannot separate our secular lives from the spiritual, because they are one and the same.

I am fed up with the mentality that everything Christian must be cheap and of low quality. Remember Solomon? He built palaces with gold and had an array of golden kitchenware! God didn't tell him that using his wealth was being carnal and he should use brass or rusted metal so people don't think he's being materialistic or covetous.

Covetousness is a heart thing. You can be rich and still be covetous. You can be poor and be covetous.

Let's not buy the lie that we can be shoddy and still represent heaven. Excuse me, but the streets of heaven are made with pure gold. There's order, hierarchy, and excellence in heaven. There's a purpose for everything, including time. God is never prodigal with His resources. Think excellence and honor. Do everything excellently and give God the glory for it.

For me, I now feel secure I can write in my own unique way, yet not to solely please anyone (though I have a target audience in mind) or with polished speeches and the latest philosophy try to impress people, because it does nothing other than merely entertain. But when I follow God's leading and directions and apply my knowledge of writing, I pray my message would be sure to bless someone.

God didn't allow you and me to go to school so we can write bad English; nor did He bless us with a talent so we can leave Him out of the equation. I have no other message to write other than to be a blessing to someone, so I have to deliberately marry these two skills.

When I write or find myself in any other vocation, I think of beauty and glory. I think of giving God the glory and being a blessing to someone. And so should you.

PONDER THIS:

Do what you know to do in the best way that not only pleases God but also helps people see Christianity the right way. An excellent way! God will be mightily pleased.

TWENTY-ONE
ORDINARY PEOPLE

An ordinary life,
Birthing kings and priests.
An ordinary death,
Birthing life everlasting.
An ordinary me,
Reaching for the stars.

AGAIN, I AM reminded of God's faithfulness. I'm definitely not the same person today that I was at the beginning of the year. I've learned so much about myself through God's Word and through writing.

So what's this chapter about? People. We are as complicated as we are ordinary. Have you ever profiled someone and filed him or her away in a tiny little compartment of your opinion? Have you ever judged someone by what they look like, where they're from, what they do for a living, how they speak, if they smile or frown, or perhaps you read their body language wrong? I have done so a million and one times. Not a nice thing I assure you.

Sometimes the noisiest people with flamboyant personalities are not necessarily the nicest people. And sometimes the quiet ones are not always the deepest thinkers. You just can't know unless you're a spiritual psychoanalyst.

Too many times we position ourselves as psychoanalysts. We assume so much about people and complicate things. Well after I made many wrong assumptions about others, I've come to assume that people are quite ordinarily the same. Environment, circumstances, other people complicate us. Peel off the many layers of riches or perceived wealth, education, social status, race, gender . . . the list goes on . . . and you will find Tom to be as ordinary as Harry. Aside from a few distinguishing differences like gender, we all are quite ordinarily the same, though not uniform.

While we pile on more things like riches, academic status, and other titles we use to define ourselves, it doesn't change who we are on the inside. We're still basically the very same people we started out with. We may react differently to others, situations, or circumstances, but we are still basically who we are. Beneath the many things we pile on ourselves for recognition, God sees the essential person inside. That's how He deals with us, because that's how He sees us.

The average, ordinary person doesn't feel comfortable around other ordinary people, perhaps because they think ordinary people are boring or pretentious. They are justified in thinking that way because they have defined ordinariness to include ways society treats "other ordinary people" deemed extra-ordinary.

If owning lots of cars is a sign of success, then striving to own many cars doesn't make you extra-ordinary. You're simply conforming to what "other ordinary people" deem is extra-ordinary, which is really someone's opinion about wealth and status.

Jesus's walking on water is a regular thing in heaven, the world to come. He suspended the present physical law to temporarily introduce a higher law. His walking on water is a miracle to us because it doesn't conform to the current laws that govern the earth. But to Jesus, it is an ordinary, everyday event.

Let me further break this down so I can swoop in for a landing.

Every casket about to be lowered into the earth houses the carcass of a being in his or her true state. At that moment, the "things" gathered over the years don't count. What counts is who he or she really was, what he or she accomplished on the inside, and whom this person affected while here on earth. It becomes that simple. Why do we complicate life so? God reiterates in the scriptures that we were created to give God pleasure.

The extra-ordinary in us should be God not things; otherwise, it all becomes meaningless when death comes calling.

As much as I love and admire people who have achieved great things, I mean really wonderful things, I always hope what they achieved has relevance in eternity. I really hope we would see everyone as quite ordinary with an extra-ordinary oomph when they're actively connected with God.

God is the extra in our ordinary.

Ponder This:

Now you know the extra in you is God. Does that change how you view yourself and other people? It should. You're just as awesome as the next person, though with different giftings and calling. God is the extra in your ordinary. That's a comforting thought.

TWENTY-TWO
COMPOSTING THE DEAD

The place of rubbish
That men often trample on
Can yield blossoms,
The sort to garnish
A king's table.

THE PAST MUST be conquered, not romanced or ignored.

Have you ever been confronted by your past? I mean, it jumps into the bandwagon of your present, having the audacity to dictate your present with the intention to influence your future.

Here's the thing, you cannot predict your future, but you can influence how it turns out by the choices you make today.

To build a bright future, I need to deal with the past and let it go. Dealing with it doesn't mean marinating in every detail. Learn what you can, if there's anything to learn, and move on.

Sometime ago I was confronted by an issue in my past. It was something I had unconsciously left unfinished. At first I was intimidated as it spewed out every ugly detail of what I used to be and how there wasn't the remotest possibility I could ever have a glorious future.

I went along with this devilish scheme, my shoulders slumping with each hurled accusation, until a tiny ember of anger welled up inside of me. A picture of the cross of Jesus flashed in my mind, and I saw pieces of nails driven deep into the grooves of His toes. I saw my past nailed and hammered into place and fastened with chords of whips, like asps around Jesus's body, seeking to crush Him with accusations meant for me. He accepted them as though He were the guilty one.

At the last He decided the siege was over. The person I used to be was nailed with Him to the cross. The person I used to be is dead and buried. No, she didn't resurrect when Jesus lifted up out of grave clothes. The person I used to be had no relevance to the present and was not given the capacity to be resurrected. She stayed dead and buried.

This knowledge is so comforting, yet it seems at no other time have I been bombarded by people who seemed to remember only my past and refused to acknowledge the new person I am. Perhaps they also are still living in the past, and this new person is a total stranger to them?

One thing we should never do after we've moved on and are confronted with the past is to try to romance it or justify ourselves. Don't do it! The past is behind. Leave it there and step away.

Once the blood of Jesus has washed all the filth away, knowing its powerful, bleaching properties, why would we try to dredge it up?

Respect the information it harbors, use it to understand how you got where you were before you were rescued, and then move on up.

The past is as dead and brittle as autumn leaves. It can never be replanted and will never sprout. But when it decays, you can add it to compost to spring new life.

Whatever last year did for you, or whatever you did with it, will soon belong to the past. Did it shed dry, decaying leaves? Add it to compost and get it into the ground of the new planting season so you can yield a bountiful harvest in the New Year.

Are you getting set for the *new*?

Start to compost it now.

PONDER THIS:

The past is in the past. Do you know you can move on now? Like Peter, you can be a champion the day after the night before. You can embrace a new you. Leave your pain and mistakes behind. Embrace the future today.

TWENTY-THREE
A LITTLE MUD AND SPIT

He grabbed an ounce of hope,
Spat some drops of faith,
Worked the works,
And rubbed in a ton of love.
And we called it
A miracle.

I DON'T HABITUALLY WRITE about people in my hemisphere, but I am compelled to do so now, partly because it's been nibbling at my thoughts for some days and more so because there's a lesson, I believe, to be learned.

We had this guard. He was young. He loved to read. I would often find him with a Bible, a daily devotional, and perhaps a newspaper spread out before him. He would bury his head in and devour every last page of these books.

I grinned from ear to ear when I first hired him. I was, like, "Wow, finally, a good one." But soon my wide smile faded and gradually turned into a scowl. You see, I didn't mind the Bible reading and all, but I do mind very much when his chores are left undone, and there's no apparent excuse why he cannot complete the tasks he was hired to do.

Everything looks good on the outside, yet something is not quite right.

We had a staff. A middle-aged man who loved to read. I would often find him with a Bible, a daily devotional, and perhaps a newspaper spread out before him. He would bury his head and devour every last page of these books.

I grinned from ear to ear when we first hired him. I was, like, "Wow, finally, a good one." But soon, my wide smile faded and turned into a scowl.

You see, I didn't mind the Bible reading and all, but I did mind sitting in a filthy car or riding in a car with an empty tank. And I did mind being preached to while being driven. He wasn't hired to preach to me when his work was left undone. And, please, spirits don't wash cars.

Everything looked good on the outside with these men, yet something was not quite right.

Christianity is much more practical than many people think. I used to want to float on clouds all day too, but that's not how it works, especially this side of heaven.

This is how it works: We have to work.

Christianity is as practical as respecting time, especially your boss's time. It is as practical as getting the job done at the right time.

I recall the episode of Jesus working with mundane tools, like mud and spit, to heal a man with long standing blindness.

He got a handful of mud, spat on it, worked it, and slapped it on the eye of a blind man. That was low-down, dirt practical. The job needed to be done, and He got down and dirty to do it. He did His own works, and then asked the man to go wash in the pool of Siloam. The man had a part to play too. Through all these, He demonstrated the practicality of the kingdom. (See John 9:6–7).

All He needed was a little mud and spit to restore sight to the blind. He had to get the mud, work up a good spit, rub together the spit and mud to get the right mixture, and then apply it. He could've just commanded the man's sight to be returned, but He didn't. He worked.

No matter how mundane the task is, as representatives of heaven we are expected to do it faithfully and with enough zest to convince everyone we enjoy the work. After all, we're doing it primarily for God.

Christianity is as practical as a phone call, a gift, a smile—every little thing that makes life a joy to others. It's about going the extra mile for another person. It's about putting others first.

Jesus's main preaching can be found in three chapters of Matthew, what Bible scholars call the Beatitudes. After that, He preached only in bits and pieces. The rest of His ministry was demonstrated in working of miracles.

Someone once said that some of us are so spiritual we're of no earthly use. Yup! That describes a lot of us to a tee.

Let me slang it this way: We just wanna preach till the cows come home. We don't wanna get down and dirty. Let me assure you, however, there's more mud and spit in Christendom than we think. We gotta be there for others. We gotta learn to help. We gotta be determined to go beyond the regular and do much more than is required. We gotta preach a little and live a lot more, 'cuz anyone can preach, but not everyone can live a life that preaches.

I'm speaking to myself also, because I can equally be quite impractical about things. But for His grace, I tend to think more than I act. However, I like to respect other people's time, especially when I'm being paid for it.

When God created man, He worked the mud. He didn't just speak man into being, He molded him.

The first thing our driver told me when he resumed his preaching at me was that he was a born-again child of God. I would have loved to see it in his character first and then form my own judgments. It's harder to live it, but it's a surer testimony.

If indeed we profess to be like our Master, then a little mud and spit shouldn't hurt.

Ponder This:

Don't you just wish we could all be more practical with our professions of love? Like someone helping with the laundry, the dishes, the kids, and so much more? That's love in action. Jesus showed us how. Sometimes the doing is a more effective witness than the saying. Do you not agree?

TWENTY-FOUR
THE PUPA PARTY

When the hammer
Chisels away
And leaves you
Roiling in pain,
Hang on,
For in a little while
It will chisel away
Yesterday's regrets
To unfold
The beauty
Of your life.

THE FIRST TIME I read Joyce Meyer's book *Battlefield of the Mind*, I staggered with rage. I hated that her message drilled a hole into my conscience—a huge one, like a mineshaft. Really, I struggled to finish the book. It was that good. I felt like a woman whose skirt had been whipped up by an unruly wind, exposing you-know-what. Unpalatable. Undesirable. Unequivocally, annoying exposure.

Ms. Meyer could very well have been peeling scabs off my old wounds that refused to heal properly. Nobody had ever confronted my weakness and challenged me like that before. Not ever, even through a book. And truly, I couldn't handle her TV broadcasts either.

I'd cringe and sink into my seat when she hammered on simple truths of the Bible applicable to everyday life. I couldn't handle the truth. I wanted always to excuse my shortcomings and pass off the blame to others, circumstances, my past, and more. I wanted to stay in that spiritual zone of all-is-well, never-mind-about-your-past, and not-bother-with-real-life-trifles.

But no matter how much I distanced myself, the truth would always hunt me down. I was once confronted by a friend who callously told me I was unbroken and needed God to fix me. That made me feel worse. Thank God, the Holy Spirit doesn't break us like so. He's ever so gentle and He does a thorough and perfect work.

God knew my wound was oozing with pus and needed tending. Plus, I knew in the depths of my heart that I had issues. I just didn't fancy anyone pointing it out or rubbing it in my face. I knew I needed to be delivered from myself, and I needed it done urgently. The problem was that I was too proud to ask my mentors for help. Might I say that, worse still, I was too proud to ask God for help. I was in the teaching ministry, and I assumed it was a shameful thing to ask for help when I was supposed to help others.

God knew the best way to heal and deliver me. It happened about five years later. He took me away geographical to an unfamiliar territory, and then He worked on me from the inside. I didn't know I had been delivered until I was led to admit it in front of a church audience while I was giving a testimony about something completely different.

That was when it dawned on me that I had changed. I could listen to hard teachings from Joyce Meyer and other men of God with similar messages and not feel condemned. Rather, I'd welcomed the searchlight of God's Word. I welcomed expository teachings. I felt loved rather than condemned, because I finally understood that God loves me too much to let me stay the same. He chastised and corrected me so I can be better than I was yesterday.

A friend and I were watching Joyce Meyer on the TV the other day, and I felt my friend cringing on the inside as she sank into her seat. I laughed inwardly. Yep! Been there. Done that. Got the T-shirt.

We really need to get to the stage in our spiritual lives where we're hungry for the truth, whether it favors us or not. We need to get to the point where we are humble enough to accept that we know absolutely nothing and are ready to soak up knowledge from the Word of God.

We need to get to the point where we're ready to receive correction and be chastened. If all we want is to be patted on the back all the time, then we're really not ready to leave the pupa party. And that's a sad place to be.

When the truth makes you angry and you cringe rather than sigh or be remorseful, it's a sign that nothing is about to change inside of you. You're closed up and not ready to grow up. "But strong meat belongeth to them that are of full age, even those who by reason of use have their senses exercised to discern both good and evil" (Heb 5:14). Growth can be painful, but it's a sign of life. Remember that anything that doesn't grow dies.

I'm glad that even at snail's pace, I am getting better each day.

What about you?

Ponder This:

The process of growth is often painful. Ask a teething baby. Once the tooth breaks through the gum and the pressure is relieved, smiles follow, along with the ability to chew solid food for sustenance and growth. God can use any method to help us grow. We just have to trust Him.

OF REDEMPTION, RESTORATION, AND WORSHIP

GOD REDEEMS US in in other to fully restore us to Him so that we can live the life of worship we were originally created for. We can't use sheer willpower to live a life that pleases Him. We need His grace, which we receive when we are fully restored to Him. Grace is part of the redemption package.

Sometimes I have tried to accomplish things just because I feel that I can. I move ahead without the help of the Holy Spirit. The end results have never been good. But when I acknowledge God's place in the scheme of things, I go to God first before I attempt anything.

Do you know that living a life that pleases God is an act of worship? It's far beyond the songs we sing on occasion in church. It's a whole lifestyle. God loves when we totally surrender in worship. Join me as we consider redemption, restoration, and worship.

ONE
UGLY IS BEAUTIFUL

I am beautiful
Because He loves me.
I am beautiful
Because He thinks of me.
I am beautiful
Because He made me.
I am beautiful
Because of His shed blood.

THE SPIKED WHIP came down with a loud thwack, lodging in ripped skin and muscle.

My body recoiled in shock. I flinched every time He groaned and gasped, steeling Himself against the blitz of pain. The swollen eyelids, jagged groves on His back, and bloodied floor forced me to my feet. I paced. Adrenaline coursed through my veins, sweat popping up like caterpillars on my skin.

I could have stopped the pain. All I had to do was to tell the jailors He was innocent, yet I uttered not a word. I chanced a quick glimpse at his beaten body. He looked horrible. In fact, He looked downright ugly. I turned my face away from Him. I was disgusted and nauseated. He had been reduced to a fleshy, messy rag. Gone were the tanned and muscular arms, the smooth skin, and beautiful piercing eyes. Worse still, his torturers were not done with him. It seemed they were just beginning.

At the time I rose up and gave false witnesses against Him, I had no idea the gravity of what I had done. His was to be a slow and painful death, a humiliating one for Him, who was once royalty.

The hefty men continued their barbaric barrage of torture, turned Him over several times to deliver more deathly blows.

Enough! I'd had enough! But no, the sentence read He had to be bruised, battered, and broken. Once the flesh was shredded then come the bones. That was the deal. That was the price He chose to pay. That was the cloak of ugliness He picked. He knew what He was up against when I sentenced Him, yet He said not a word.

He looked weak and ugly, and I looked away from Him.

Then He slumped.

They dragged Him back to the cell and mopped up the puddle of priceless blood. Torrents of taunts and jeers did nothing to make Him defend Himself or declare His innocence. He was paraded before a crowd of cynics, wearing a crown of thorns wedged hard into His temple.

Yet through it all, He looked at me with eyes filled with love.

"He hath no form nor comeliness; and when we shall see him, there is no beauty that we should desire him" (Isa. 53:2). I never imagined this ugly would give me a beautiful life now and in heaven thereafter. I never imagined every scar, every pain and torment, every mark from the spiked whip, every bruise, every sickness and disease meant for me, He was ready and willing to take on Himself. "But he was wounded for our transgressions, he was bruised for our iniquities: the chastisement of our peace was upon Him and with his stripes we are healed" (v. 5).

My husband handed me a damp handkerchief as we stood up. I was too sedated with anguish to notice that he was sobbing too. The words *Passion of the Christ* flashed on the large screen, followed by THE END and the credits. If I had no graphic idea just how ugly Jesus had become for my salvation, now I clearly saw.

For every ugly indentation in His body, it was to save me, give me a beautiful life.

Ugly is truly beautiful; the ugly who saved me.

Ponder This:

Jesus had a reason to leave all the beauty and glory of heaven to suffer a humiliating death. You! Did you know? He cast off His beautiful and clothed you with it. Embrace God's beauty. Embrace the life of grace. He did it all just for you.

TWO
APPROVED FOR TRAVEL

Going up yonder
To the place of bliss,
A place of peace,
With my baggage
Of accomplished dreams
And my ticket for destiny
Paid for by
The blood of Jesus.

DO YOU HAVE a passport to the place beyond?
She leafed through my passport, stamped, and returned it. Unlike the others who either have a blank or an intimidating stare, this woman from Immigration wore a compassionate look. I attributed it to the fact that she was enamored by my daughter's antics during our walk through the airport scanner.

After helping my daughter with her shoes, this woman wished us a safe flight. I ventured to ask her if she'd been anywhere herself. She shook her head. She'd never been inside of an airplane, much less flew in one anywhere. Day in day out she stamped passports, saw business executives and families head out to their various destinations for either work or pleasure. Daily she interacted or simply watched people go in and out of the departure gate but never ever saw beyond her post.

It reminded me of Paul's saying, "But I keep under my body, and bring it into subjection: lest that by any means, when I have preached to others, I myself should be a castaway" (1 Cor. 9:27).

What a tragedy to certify others fit to enter the airplane and to enter another country but never have the opportunity to travel.

It's a common tragedy, I know, but in God's kingdom it's a terrible one. Having preached salvation to others, prayed for them, healed the sick, cast out demons, performed awesome and inspiring miracles and yet never tasting the good land is a fatalistic tragedy.

So the woman checked people for qualifying documentations to grant them exit to a better place, but she herself did not possess the same qualifying documentation. "Wherefore by their fruits ye shall know them. Not every one that saith unto me, Lord, Lord, shall enter into the kingdom of heaven; but he that doeth the will of my Father which is in heaven" (Matt. 7:20–21).

We are not justified by what we know or preach but by who we are and what we practice behind closed doors. This makes me tremble as I write, knowing that at the end of the day I earnestly desire to hear not how good my writing is, what insight or the depths of what I fish out of my thoughts, or even how much it has changed, transformed, or enlightened others *but* what God thinks and says about me and if I am fulfilling my purpose. How I work out *my own* salvation with fear and trembling. Oh, to hear His words "Well done, thou good and faithful servant"!

> Wherefore seeing we also are compassed about with so great a cloud of witnesses, let us lay aside every weight, and the sin which doth so easily beset us, and let us run with patience the race that is set before us, Looking unto Jesus the author and finisher of our faith; who for the joy that was set before him endured the cross, despising the shame, and is set down at the right hand of the throne of God. (Heb. 12:1–2)

As we look to living an altruistic life, one of service to others, we need to do a periodic stocktaking of our spiritual walk with God. Is it God-ward or man-ward? Do we live to please others to the detriment of our faith or do we live to please God in spite of it all? The Bible tells us how in these versions of 2 Corinthians 13:5: Examine yourselves, whether ye be in the faith; prove your own selves. Examine and test and evaluate your own selves to see whether you are holding to your faith and showing the proper fruits of it. Test and prove yourselves. (AMP)

Test yourselves to make sure you are solid in the faith. Don't drift along taking everything for granted. Give yourselves regular check-ups. You need firsthand evidence, not mere hearsay that Jesus Christ is in you.

> Test it out. If you fail the test, do something about it. I hope the test won't show that we have failed. But if it comes to that, we'd rather the test showed our failure than yours. We're rooting for the truth to win out in you. We couldn't possibly do otherwise."
>
> (vv. 5–7 MSG).

At the end of the day, what matters the most is the life that pleases God.

Ponder This:

Have you ever tried to please God on your own terms and in your own way? Just like the woman in this story, the prerequisite to pleasing God is faith—faith in God and His Word. Do you need faith? Get some from the Bible.

THREE
THE GENTLE CROONER

His voice is gentle,
Soothing and endearing.
His voice is patient,
Longing and imploring.
His voice is captivating,
Assuring and restoring.

WE ONCE HAD a landline phone at home that crooned when we switched it on and gave an even longer symphony when its battery was flat and dying out.

Although the sound irritated me because it was so loud and could set off at any time, especially at night when all was still and quiet, the good thing was that it alerted me to quickly plug it back into its source of energy.

Don't you wish you had an alert like that for when things are about to fall flat in your face? An alert that tells us something is about to go wrong, so we can quickly plug back into our source. Samson ignored the bleeps of his alert within until he could hear it no more. "And she said, The Philistines be upon thee, Samson. And he awoke out of his sleep, and said, I will go out as at other times before, and shake myself. And he wist [knew] not that the LORD was departed from him" (Judg. 16:20).

Samson had no clue he was alone. That is so scary . . . when you think you're covered on all fronts, only to realize too late that you are indeed naked and exposed.

When the Spirit of Grace comes, He comes with power, but when He leaves (because He's a perfect gentleman), He leaves ever so quietly. You will hardly notice He's gone.

Look at what happened on the Day of Pentecost:

> And when the day of Pentecost was fully come, they were all with one accord in one place. And suddenly there came a *sound* from heaven as of a *rushing mighty wind*, and it filled the entire house where they were sitting. And there appeared unto them *cloven tongues like as of fire*, and it sat upon each of them. And they were all filled with the Holy Ghost, and began to *speak with other tongues*, as the Spirit gave them utterance. And there were dwelling at Jerusalem Jews, devout men, out of every nation under heaven. Now when this was *noised abroad,* the multitudes came together, and were confounded, because that every man heard them speak in his own language. And they were all amazed and marveled, saying one to another, Behold, are not all these which speak Galilaeans? (Acts 2:1–7 Author's emphasis)

Please take note of the emphasized words. The impact of the presence of the Holy Spirit was felt *everywhere*. Does that mean we don't get an alert prior to His withdrawal from active participation in our lives if we were to frustrate or ignore His presence, so to speak? Of course not! Samson had multiple alerts, but he gave in to his weaknesses.

We often get that voice of conscience, that tug at our hearts, that discomfort in our spirits, and that feeling something is not quite right.

When praise, prayer, and His presence no longer hold any appeal to us, and there's no fire burning inside to pursue Him, we've missed the "crooning."

To get us back on track, God may speak through a person, a friend, a family member, a pastor, a TV program, a book, a devotional, or a circumstance or situation. He will try to get our attention to check ourselves and get plugged back to our source. God will do everything to get our attention.

But when we ignore the repeated warnings, everything we once held dear loses meaning, and sin lures us, we begin to dance to its tune. It's downhill thereon.

When other Christians start to irritate us or sound holier than thou, and gossip magazines or soap operas seem much more interesting than the Bible, something is wrong . . . very wrong. We are at ease with sin, and so we ought to be afraid.

We cannot separate God from His character and His Word. If He says He cannot abide with sin, He means it and will not compromise His standard for you, His beloved.

Sin punches a gaping hole in the hedge around us, inviting a steady stream of devils into our lives. And, sadly, we would not know when the Spirit of Grace leaves. Like Samson, we would stumble around blindly, flexing muscles, thinking and believing all is well. May that not be our portion in Jesus's name. Amen.

Even if we have missed it, God can and will restore us back to Him. God's assurance is this:

> The LORD has appeared of old to me, saying: "I have loved you with an everlasting love; Therefore with lovingkindness I have drawn you. Again I will build you, and you shall be rebuilt, O virgin of Israel! You shall again be adorned with your tambourines, and shall go forth in the dances of those who rejoice. You shall yet plant vines on the mountains of Samaria." (Jer. 31:3–5a NKJV)

God is willing to work with and within us to get us back on track. He wants to rebuild all our broken walls and adorn us with His goodness, favor, mercy, and blessings.

There's much more than physical prosperity in His presence. The Devil has an idea of what we stand to gain. If it weren't worth it, he wouldn't work so hard to keep us from God's presence and cause us to rationalize our way out of grace.

Are you getting an alert to plug back into your source or go deeper with Him today? It doesn't matter what stage you're at. God is ready to restore and rebuild. In His presence is fullness of joy, and at His right hand are pleasures evermore.

The Holy Spirit is here to help us get back to God, and He will do it again and again, but He won't force us. He's a perfect gentleman. He extends His hands. I will take them. Will you?

Ponder This:

God extends salvation through His grace. It's free to be saved. Someone paid the price already. Wouldn't you like to access this free gift?

FOUR
SPEED

Hurry!
There's a race
To the finish line.
Leave your cloak
And your load behind.
The Savior is
Cheering you on.

O N ONE OF those rare times since becoming a mum, I got to watch a movie, *Speed* with Keanu Reeves and Sandra Bullock. I know it's old, released in 1994, but it was my first time watching it and I liked it. What I particularly liked about *Speed* had nothing to do with its theatrics or the cast; the plot got me all fired up.

(Please note this spoiler alert as I take you through the movie and draw parallels with our walk with the Lord.)

A disgruntled retired cop-cum-psychopath, whom I'll call Baddie, demanded a sum of money from the LAPD for being retired unjustly. He threatened to blow up a bus if his demands were not met. He happened to pick Keanu Reeves (police officer Jack) to convey his message. He placed a bomb on a city bus, which must keep traveling above fifty miles per hour (eighty km/h) or the bomb would explode. Being the humanistic person he was, Keanu got on the bus, hoping to save the lives of the passengers.

Imagine driving a bus at fifty miles per hour on a freeway, without stopping, even with traffic in the way.

Here lies the challenge: the bus must continue at this rate of speed no matter what. The first huddle was internal. The passengers argued and complained about one another. In the face of a serious issue, their true natures unraveled. As a result, Baddie shot the driver, so Sandra was forced to take control of the wheels.

From then, things spiraled out of control. I would have thought the passengers would have found a way to band together.

Differences and dissentions are the first sign of bull's-eyes in any group of people. Pull them apart and you can conquer them. Guess what? That's what the Devil looks for in any group of Christians: dissensions and disagreements.

The second hurdle in *Speed* was traffic up ahead. Good thing they had the police headquarters behind them and a helicopter hovering above, giving minute by minute guidance on which freeways to take and the routes to avoid. At some point they went on a bridge under construction and had to brace themselves for a crash. For a split second they fought together, staring possible death in the face. Sandra floored the accelerator, and they made it over the broken bridge.

The Lord sees ahead of us, and when it seems bleak and we are confused, He shows us which way to go to arrive at our destination.

The wounded bus driver in the movie was bleeding, and after negotiations Baddie agreed to let the man off the bus. Unknown to other passengers, however, a woman was determined to get off the bus at the same time. She didn't want to die. As a police truck pulled adjacent to the bus to haul the wounded man in, the petrified woman followed suit, even when Baddie gave the strict instruction that no one other than the wounded driver was to get off the bus.

Fear took hold of her, and as she was about to leave the bus, Baddie blew her away. Strange thing is that she was the only one who died.

Fear is a terrible thing. It makes us irrational.

The only way forward for the rushing bus and captive passengers from then on was the airfield. They would just circle around and around until the police worked out a solution. However, the problem was they were running out of fuel, which meant they would eventually slow down, drop below the mandated fifty miles per hour, and thus trigger the bomb.

Fast-forward.

Reeves and Bullock discovered Baddie had installed a camera on the bus, so every time they had devised a plan, Baddie was on to it and was two steps ahead of them.

Some quick thinking and a few minutes later, they got everyone off the bus except Sandra, who had to steer the bus, and Keanu, who had to stay with her. Eventually, they jumped out as it crashed into a stationary plane.

Lots of loud explosions, and fireballs followed.

Phew! That was great.

We feel that way when we've just come out of some crisis, overcome a challenge, or solved a complicated problem. We breathe a sigh of relief and feel reinvigorated. Some people may feel on top of the world, some may ask "Why did it have to happen to me?", and others may wish it never happens again.

The truth is that crisis is as common to life as the air we breathe. Sorry, mate. No smooth sailing. We're either heading toward a crisis or coming out of one.

Back to our movie. Now everyone is safe and sound, but Baddie is still at large. What to do? The crack LAPD team pursued Baddie to a supposed location. But Keanu understood Baddie's thinking and knew they were on a wild goose chase.

The team was blown to smithereens when they swooped into Baddie's former lodging. This hunt for Baddie no longer had anything to do with Keanu. He could easily have gone home in the ambulance, but the lawman in him wouldn't let up. Besides, if he left, Baddie would still be free to continue his killing ways.

Just because we overcome one issue doesn't mean that's it. And sometimes it could be a brother, a sister, or close friend who needs help. We've had our crisis, overcome it, and learned something from it. That's what qualifies us to help others. Compassion should be our driving force.

When Keanu left Sandra in the ambulance to help his colleagues,

Baddie showed up from seemingly nowhere and stole Sandra away. He strapped her with all kinds of bombs and led her down an alley into an underground train station.

Keanu discovered this and went after them. At that moment, because of their common experience, Keanu had developed feelings for Sandra and watched, tortured because he couldn't stop Baddie from taking Sandra onto a train.

Just when we feel we've reached the end of our ordeal, the Devil springs another surprise. It seems as though we're living from crisis to crisis. Actually, as long as we are God-chasers, we've been enlisted in an army. The battle is ongoing. We may lose some battles and we may win some, but the war was already won 2000 years ago.

At this point in the movie, I felt nervous and frustrated that Baddie seemed to have the upper hand.

Baddie tied Sandra to a pole, killed the train conductor, and left the train on full speed, with the intention to crash it once he had safely made it out with his ransom loot. But when he discovered that the money delivered by the police was only loose pieces of paper, he lost his temper.

Meanwhile, Keanu got atop the train and tried to rescue Sandra, but with all the gizmos strapped to her body, it was impossible to defuse the contraption within the short amount of time ticking down on the timer.

Baddie showed up, and the two men fought it out atop the train until Baddie lost his head, literally.

At this point, I screamed, "Woo hoo!"

Keanu scuttled back into the train and deactivated the bomb strapped on Sandra, but he couldn't unlock the handcuff that held her to the pole as the train raced down the track. So he tried to stop the train, but realized neither the speedometer nor the accelerator worked, and the train, traveling at a high speed, was headed for a construction site. Wowzers!

Life! Huh? Some troubles are just like that speeding train, hurtling you into the worst kind of nightmare.

Keanu and Sandra held on for dear life, knowing that this time they wouldn't make it. How do you stop a speeding train heading for nowhere?

Well, it's a movie, and I can say that by sheer providence or luck, they crashed into the city center unhurt, kissing, laughing, and feeling happy.

In the life of a believer, this kind of thing is called divine intervention. I imagined angels gently bearing and guiding that train until it came to a stop. It's easy to watch a film, and despite all the tossing and turning, there's always the assurance the actor will make it. We enjoy the thrill, the danger, and still know our heroes will be saved somehow.

In real life we can have the same assurance that, come what may, God's got our backs. No matter the situation, as long as we stand firm, God always comes through for us, even to death.

The victory in the life of a believer is that God has us engraved on the palm of His hands, and He allows only what constitutes His will to occur in our lives.

I may not be in a speeding train with a time bomb strapped to my body, but when life straps danger to me, I know angels are at work around me, keeping me in all my ways.

In the face of the current crisis in the country, God will keep and preserve you. He never sleeps nor slumbers. His angels watch over us every fraction of a second.

God's speed to you.

Ponder This:

Do you know God's angels watch over you day and night? Not one moment do they take their eyes from you. Isn't that comforting?

FIVE
A PRISON BREAK AT CHRISTMAS

T'was for me He died,
T'was my pain He bore,
'Tis the reason I live
Every Christmas morn.

MY INTENTION WAS to watch a feel-good movie with my hubby, something we hadn't done in almost two years since our daughter's birth. And I'm not the type to watch a movie in silence. I run commentaries throughout, and it frustrates Hubby. I mean, I literally rewrite the script as I watch, and I ask a million questions or make contentious statements.

I was confident this would be a regular action-packed movie with a lot of good twists. We slotted in the DVD and watched the show *Prison Break* from one episode to another, one season to another. I was struck by the captivating plot, the twists and turns, and the theme of the movie; the inherent power of love one man had for his brother.

Here's a quick summary of the movie (*spoiler alert*).

Due to a political conspiracy, an innocent man (Lincoln) is sent to death row and is incarcerated in a penitentiary where he awaits his execution. His only hope is his brother (Scofield), a brilliant structural engineer who is convinced of his brother's innocence and makes it his mission to deliberately get himself sent to the same prison in order to break out both of them by cleverly devised, elaborate plans.

I watched with dismay as Scofield, an innocent man, plants himself in prison, roughs it out with other inmates with one singular purpose: to break himself and his brother out of the well-manned fortress. One plan after the other fails, and it seems they would never get out of the prison.

Throughout their planning and eventual escape, I had moments when it was impossible to run a commentary. I was petrified for them. I felt their fear, racing hearts, and constant looking over the shoulder.

As the episodes rolled one into the other, I couldn't help but admire and be deeply touched by Scofield's devotion to his brother. He seemed unfazed by the discomfort of the prison, the harassment of fellow inmates, the possibility of their plans falling through, or being caught after escaping. He just couldn't bear the thought of his brother dying.

In the end, Scofield died to free his brother and wife. He gave his life for them.

I sobbed at the depth of his feelings and wondered if this kind of love truly existed in real life.

Then it hit me.

The only time I can think of such a powerful, perfect, passionate, delicate, and committed love for another was when Jesus planted himself in this fallen world. In order to free me from prison, He had to become a prisoner Himself. In order to remove my shackles, He had to wear shackles. In order to remove my pain, He had to take my pain on Himself. In order to heal me, He had to become diseased.

This verse sums it up beautifully: "But he was wounded for our transgressions, he was bruised for our iniquities: the chastisement of our peace was upon him; and with his stripes we are healed" (Isa. 53:5).

Someone loved me enough to walk in my shoes. Someone loved me enough to die for me. Someone loved me enough to save me. Someone loved me enough to free me.

Think with me for a minute, will you?

He left the grandeur of heaven: "And now, Father, glorify Me along with Yourself and restore Me to such majesty and honor in Your presence as I had with You before the world existed" (John 17:5 AMP).

He robed Himself in human flesh: "And He took with Him Peter and James and John, and began to be struck with terror and amazement and deeply troubled and depressed" (Mark 14:33 AMP).

He came from the poorest family and took on the lowest form of employment, such that others disdained Him: "Is not this the carpenter, the son of Mary, the brother of James, and Joses, and of Judas, and Simon? and are not his sisters here with us? And they were offended at him" (Mark 6:3).

He was birthed in the lowliest place: "And she brought forth her firstborn son, and wrapped him in swaddling clothes, and laid him in a manger; because there was no room for them in the inn" (Luke 2:7).

He died the most unjust and humiliating death just to save me. They crucified Him like a criminal: "Two other men, both criminals, were also led out with him to be executed. When they came to the place called the Skull, they crucified him there, along with the criminals—one on his right, the other on his left" (Luke 23:32–33 NIV).

He suffered separation from God, the Father: "And at the ninth hour Jesus cried with a loud voice, saying, Eloi, Eloi, lama sabachthani? which is, being interpreted, My God, my God, why hast thou forsaken me?" (Mark 15:34).

He went down to hell and hades to ensure not just my freedom from the evil one but my place beside Him on the throne for eternity: "For thou wilt not leave my soul in hell; neither wilt thou suffer thine Holy One to see corruption" (Ps. 16:10; see Acts 2:27).

Jesus knew what it would take, yet He willingly paid the price. He came into my prison cell, wore the same prison clothes, ate the same prison food, took on burdens and tasks, bore the harassment of the wardens and guards, underwent twenty-four-hour surveillance for one singular purpose: *to set me free. I am free indeed.*

Ponder This:

Are you free? Do you daily appreciate what it cost Jesus to purchase your freedom? If you're not yet free, would you like to be? Jesus is waiting just for you.

SIX
CHANGE? NO, NOT ME

Change my works,
Lift them with grace.
Change my words,
Fill them with faith.
Change my heart,
Let it love you more.
Change my life
Even as You change not.

I HATE IT, HATE it, *hate it*. I am just getting to understand my computer and its intricate workings. The codes, the symbols, the commands, the nuances, and the idiosyncrasies overwhelm me. I am just getting to understand all these complexities and how to work it to make me a genius. I am about to master this device, subdue it, dominate it, and push it to make me produce, multiply, and replenish spent and exhausted creativity.

And just when I figure it out, a new version is released. A new model fashioned and patterned after a new ideology and think tank. A dreaded notice to update crops up. Alas, I am tossed into the throes of new learning and new skills.

And just when the romance begins, and we start a waltz and tango down the bridge of familiarity; when we begin to complete each other's sentences via auto-complete, and I no longer need to synonym-ize, wham! I am hit in the face with the newest latest version of the last latest version, which has suddenly become the old version.

I love change, but not like this. Not when it alters my path for no good reason. Not when it takes the zest out of spontaneous creativity. I want to write, not read codes and codecs. I want to dream, not read how to dream.

But I am glad that when I consult the manual of life, God's love letter to me, its timeless charges and principles remain the same. He never ever changes His mind about His love for me. I don't have to live in fear that maybe God has had a rethink and commanded some prophets to rewrite the Bible with the clause indicating that, perhaps, I am only a conditional favorite.

Come rain or shine, even when my emotions vary, I look into the mirror of His Word and am reminded time and again just how crazy He is about me. When everything else is changing, God's love is like an anchor in the midst of the storm. It stills everything, even change.

God's love is timeless, boundless, and ageless; and it transcends the latest technology of zillions of years to come. God is the only constant I know, the unchangeable changer. "For I am the LORD, I change not; therefore ye sons of Jacob are not consumed" (Mal. 3:6).

What changes is His revelation of Himself to me. In that case, I love change.

PONDER THIS:

What about you? How do you react to change? Does it delight you, though God's Word never changes? Does it thrill you even more that God's love for you never changes?

SEVEN
TILT TO THE LIGHT

A little tilt
To the way of life
Is like a little light
In the midst of darkness.
It shines ever so bright,
No matter how small the light.

LATELY I HAVE had to be on a probiotic supplement. Apart from being a digestive elixir, probiotic is an enzyme (I'm not a chemist, so I hope I'm correct with my terminology) that introduces good bacteria (flora) into the body. Our bodies contain billions of both good and bad bacteria. A tilt in the equilibrium determines ill health or good health. When the bad bacteria outweigh the good bacteria, we fall ill. It means we don't have enough good bacteria to combat the bad bacteria. Probiotic contains billions of good bacteria that help to reinforce, fortify, and replenish good bacteria in the body's system. It therefore strengthens the immune system and helps fight most diseases naturally.

Although we're in the world, we stand at great risk if we let the world system (bad bacteria) surpass the Word of God (good bacteria) in our lives. We watch television, listen to unsavory gossip, read magazines and books that introduce lifestyles that oppose the Word of God; therefore, we become weak in faith and see every problem as a death sentence rather than an exploit of faith. We can undo this by introducing the Bible (good bacteria) to choke the worldliness in our systems. All it takes is just a little tilt in the right direction.

At the onset of the year, when I realized I had too much bad stuff in me, I decided to tilt toward the light by reintroducing the cleansing Word of God. A good shock to the system, I daresay. And I'll admit that serious Bible study is not easy.

Are you like me? I start reading from Genesis, Exodus, skip Leviticus, and jump to Numbers? I just can't get all the terminology into my medulla oblongata. But His grace is sufficient. The more we get into the Bible, the thirstier we get, and God unfolds His Word to us and bring new knowledge to light.

You too can tilt toward the light. There's so much bad bacteria in our world. Don't get swallowed up in the hopelessness of it all.

"This book of the law shall not depart out of thy mouth; but thou shalt meditate therein day and night, that thou mayest observe to do according to all that is written therein: for then thou shalt make thy way prosperous, and then thou shalt have good success" (Josh. 1:8).

Ponder This:

A little tilt toward God is all we need. Afterward, His grace bears us up like wings. Have you tilted yet?

EIGHT
THE SQUALL

Tempests beckon
To His whispers.
Mountains hasten
To His presence.
How majestic is
The Lord our God.

I WAS UP AT 2 a.m. I had a lot on my mind. I had prayer points. I was teaming up with someone to meet with the Lord at this time. I looked out the window, and though it was dark, I felt a kind of brightness in the atmosphere. Not one that I can describe, but it didn't feel so dark. As soon as I began praying, the wind wafted outside. I was glad. Welcome rain—it'd been so hot. The drops turned into a torrent and the downpour barraged my windows. I had to raise my voice a little so I could hear myself.

The fellowship was great.

I remembered when I used to be obsessed with what God's voice sounded like. I read in the Bible that it sounded like the voice of many waters: "And I heard a voice from heaven, as the voice of many waters, and as the voice of a great thunder" (Rev. 14:2a).

My imagination would go wild. Would His voice be loud? Formidable? Awesome? The list goes on.

As I prayed, lightning streaked across the sky like silver-white wiry fingers. I was blinded momentarily. I closed my eyes to preserve their sensitivity and felt my way around the room. Suddenly, a thunderous sound shattered the silence of the night. I hadn't heard booming thunder like this in a long time. I shuddered a bit and ran to rescue my daughter from her room, where she whimpered.

After putting her down on my bed, I resumed my praying. Believe it or not, a loud sound, almost out of this world, came from the sky—a mix of thunder and lightning. And I almost jumped out of my skin.

Like I said, I hadn't experienced the typical African thunderstorm in a while, so this one took me by surprise. I was bothered that it got to me; even the next clap of thunder and the next one. Okay, funny bit is, I had to rebuke the spirit of fear. Do I scare easily? No. But again, I repeat, this one got to me. It was so loud and penetrating I thought it could rip the house off of its foundation.

Then I remembered my past ruminations about the voice of God; like the sound of great thunder. Hmmm, if this African thunder got to me, I can only imagine the voice of our great God. This thunder was just a simile of the real deal: The Voice of God Like Thunder.

This is the God we serve. The God whose voice alone can only be likened to thunder, because there's nothing else we can compare it with. This is the God who fights for us. How can the enemy hear His voice and not die of fright? It reminds me of one of my favorite psalms:

> Then the earth shook and trembled; the foundations also of the hills moved and were shaken, because he was wroth. There went up a smoke out of his nostrils, and fire out of his mouth devoured: coals were kindled by it. He bowed the heavens also, and came down: and darkness was under his feet. And he rode upon a cherub, and did fly: yea, he did fly upon the wings of the wind. He made darkness his secret place; his pavilion round about him were dark waters and thick clouds of the skies. At the brightness that was before him his thick clouds passed, hail stones

and coals of fire. The LORD also thundered in the heavens, and the Highest gave his voice; hail stones and coals of fire. Yea, he sent out his arrows, and scattered them; and he shot out lightnings, and discomfited them. Then the channels of waters were seen, and the foundations of the world were discovered at thy rebuke, O LORD, at the blast of the breath of thy nostrils. He sent from above, he took me, he drew me out of many waters. He delivered me from my strong enemy, and from them which hated me: for they were too strong for me. They prevented me in the day of my calamity: but the Lord was my stay. He brought me forth also into a large place; he delivered me, because he delighted in me. (18:7–19)

This selection of the Psalms pictorially describes God's anger against our enemies. If you don't fear God yet, please, I employ you to read the entire Psalm 18 again and again. I'd rather be on the side of a God, whose blast of the breath of His nostrils alone can uproot the foundations of the earth.

What an awesome God we serve!

PONDER THIS:

God can be as tender as He is formidable. He commands awe and honor. Sometimes we take His tenderness and grace for granted. Sometimes we forget He's on our side. Sometimes we forget He places mercy before judgment. Sometimes we forget He just wants to love us.

NINE
MY NAME IN NEON LIGHTS

Twinkle, twinkle, little light,
Blazing pathways through the dark,
Sifting true and tender hearts,
Engraving names with bloody ink.

I LOVE SEEING MY name in the lights, most especially neon lights. It's a testament of having done or achieved or being recognized for something great. I saw my name in . . . well, not neon lights but on a FedEx package. It felt good, though, to know someone thought of me and wrote my name, not in ink but in handwritten letters on a brown cardboard box. Never mind that it was an order I had placed and purchased with my own money.

But listen, the most important place to see your name written is in the Lamb's Book of Life, carefully, lovingly, and tenderly written by our Savior, who shed His precious blood.

Names written in neon lights may count for a season. They will fizzle away with a dying trend, but those written in this Book of Life count for eternity. Do you have your name written in blood in the Lamb's Book of Life? "And whosoever was not found written in the book of life was cast into the lake of fire" (Rev. 20:15); "And there shall in no wise enter into it any thing that defileth, neither whatsoever worketh abomination, or maketh a lie: but they which are written in the Lamb's book of life" (21:27).

PONDER THIS:

The best place to have your name listed is in the Lamb's Book of Life.

TEN

HAVE YOU MET MY SON?

Have you met Jesus?
Have you heard of the Cross?
Have you seen the nail-pierced hands?
Have you been washed in His blood?
Have you received life eternal?
Are you being called His own?

WHEN MY DAUGHTER first started to read, she read from one of her bedtime Bible stories, and when she got to the part where it said that Jesus was God's Son, she said, "Huh! God has a Son?"

I nodded. Frown lines creased her cute little forehead, and her eyes took on the faraway look that often makes me utter, "Uh oh."

I imagined the wheels in her head turning, playing Pythagorean theorem and simple logic, wondering how come God has a Son.

Normally she would have probed further, but for some reason, which elated me, she didn't. I think, however, that she filed that information away for the future. I'm quite sure I haven't heard the last of that question just yet.

It made me think too.

God has a Son. His name is Jesus. The Jesus factor is what makes the difference between a born-again child of God and the regular Mr.

Joe Bloggs Christian down the road. God is universally accepted in most places and among all religions of the world, but introduce the Jesus factor and the story changes.

I remember seeing an imposing billboard hoisted on a four-story building bang in the middle of Jibowu as you descend the Ojuelegba Bridge leading toward Ikorodu Road. Lagosians would know this route. And you might have even seen it yourself if you ply that route often. In bold red letters against a white backdrop it read: Have You Met My Son Jesus? Signed, God.

You can't miss the billboard as you descend the bridge. The first time I saw it I was overwhelmed. Not quite sure which church or person paid for the bold advert, but I was thanking God for them. The words gave me goose pimples.

It felt like the River Jordan experience, at least to my mind. I could almost hear God's voice booming, "This is my beloved Son in whom I am well pleased."

Indeed, Father God is well pleased with Jesus, the plan of redemption, the ultimate sacrifice on the cross, and the yielding of many sons, like you and me and many more for whom the Lord died. Father God is pleased with us who have been redeemed because of the blood. We've been raised to the same status as Christ, made to sit in heavenly places with Him.

For anyone reading this who doesn't have this same privilege, my question to you is, have you met Jesus? God would ask the same question of you. How can anyone reject such a precious gift as Jesus? Perhaps because they haven't met Him yet.

For God so loved you that He gave His only begotten son, Jesus, that if you would take that step and accept Him as your Lord and Savior, you shall be saved from damnation and saved for eternity with God.

Ponder This:

Have you met Jesus?

ELEVEN

TLC

Tender Lord
Loving Father
Caring Master

GOD'S HEART POUNDS with our worship. When our praise fills His temple, a powerful anointing flows from His presence. And where God's anointing is, every yoke is destroyed. (See Isaiah 10:27.)

God desires our worship, our praise, and our adoration much more than our works of righteousness. I want to worship and praise God with all my heart. Will you join me in a little TLC?

How am I even capable of loving God by myself without His infusing in me with the ability to love Him out of the abundant love He poured into me? "Because the love of God is shed abroad in our hearts by the Holy Ghost which is given unto us" (Rom. 5:5).

I never once believed it is easy to love God. Although we were created for His praise, to love and worship Him, we naturally gravitate toward self-centeredness, self-delusion, self-sufficiency, self-preservation, and self-love because we are only interested in ourselves. Without God's given ability to love, we cannot love. In my own strength, of my own capability I cannot love even God. That's why I am Thirsty, Longing, and Chasing (TLC) after Him. "As the hart panteth for the water brooks, so panteth my soul for Thee, O God" (Ps. 42:1).

My soul is parched and thirsty for you, Lord. Just as the deer, my tongue is swollen and gummed to the roof of my mouth. I hear the gurgling of pure, clean, refreshing water in the distance. I gallop with clumsy hooves and bound straight for the water of life. I am thirsty, longing, and chasing after life. I know one gulp alone can refresh me, though I need more and more of an endless supply. "Spread out my hands to You; My soul longs for You like a thirsty land" (143:6).

With outstretched hands, I soak in the refreshing water of life. The deadness within the soil revives. Dry bones clink and receive life. I'm alive again. I can breathe His life.

I cannot love God as I ought and in my strength because I just cannot. It amazes me to know that God loves me immeasurably and immensely. The universe is sustained by His love. Gravity is dynamism of His love. The planets spin in their orbit without any thought of collision with one another. The seas rage and roar and yet never roll beyond the sandy shores. The seasons spin from one to the other, on time and on cue. Seeds drop by either design or carelessness, yet they contain the DNA to reproduce after their kind, and they sink deep down, germinate, and sprout new life. How can I not Thirst, Long, and Chase after God? "O God, You are my God; Early will I seek You; My soul thirsts for You; My flesh longs for You In a dry and thirsty land Where there is no water" (63:1).

Everywhere you look, humankind fights against and denies the existence of God. Everyone struggles to be self-sufficient and self-sustaining. As for me, I am helpless without God. I cannot see my way without His guiding light. I cannot live without His love. I cannot move without His protection. I cannot create without His inspiration. I cannot help but lean on His grace. I cannot help but Thirst, Long, and Chase after God. And for everyone who is thirsty, God reaches out to quench his or her thirst. "For I will pour water on him who is thirsty" (Isa. 44:3).

Daily His grace and mercy astound me. God has been so good to me. But I have fallen short of His glory a trillion times, yet His grace and mercy reach out, restore, and refresh my soul. That is why I cannot stop Thirsting, Longing, and Chasing after God.

"The parched ground shall become a pool, and the thirsty land springs of water" (35:7). Even in arid situations, hopelessness, and seemingly impossible dryness, God causes the rain—a cool refreshing pool right where the ground used to be cracked and crumbly and dry. right where all living creatures had either crawled away or singed and charred in the searing heat of the merciless sun. Right there where death stank, right there, God splashes a pool of glistening, cool, reviving water. Right where the land snuffed breath out of its former occupants, God bursts out a spring of water. How refreshing is His presence! How soothing is His Loving-kindness. That is why I'm Thirsty, Longing, and Chasing after God. "For He satisfies the longing soul, And fills the hungry soul with goodness" (Ps. 107:9).

On the day I cried out earnestly, and with slurred speech mouthed His name, I was filled with an intense longing for His presence. His joy overwhelmed me as I burst out with praise. He is worthy of every ounce of praise, every iota of worship; every fiber of strength to dance before His throne; every bead of sweat; every thump of a racing, anxious heart; every nimble foot; every outstretched hand; every orchestrated beat, toe-tap, hand-clap, head-sway, bend-low; every move; every thought; every word; every tune in every way . . . just to praise His holy name. He is worthy, and so I am Thirsty, Longing, and Chasing after God.

He honors every grasp for His presence, every heart filled with hope. He fills me to overflowing with His goodness, His very best, and His unspeakable joy.

What about you? Do you pant after Him and long to be in His presence? Is God worth *everything* to you?

Ponder This:

Worship is the best way to get into and stay in God's presence.

BEFORE YOU GO

HAVE YOU EVER wondered why the universe and its entire majestic span rotates without tiring? How it all fits together? How the stars and planets respect the boundaries so that they don't collide with one another? Or how gravity sucks us right back to earth, and we're not flung around in space? What about the expanse of the oceans that stays shy of the shorelines? There's a God in heaven who makes all these things fit perfectly.

As enormous as the heavenly bodies are and intricate in design, and compared with a tiny strand of hair on our heads, God cares about you, and He loves you enough to leave all of heaven to come down to earth to die a sinner's death just for you. Life has never made more sense than when one lives it in Christ. An account of many people on their death beds often indicate the regrets they have of life is almost always about love and value rather than riches and fame. People often wished they loved more or gave more but don't regret that they didn't amass more wealth.

Are you saved? It's a question we will all have to answer here now or there then. Jesus came to earth to die like a common criminal to redeem you and me that we may have our names written in the Lamb's Book of Life, and counted as worthy to live and reign with Christ throughout eternity. Life—no matter how long it is—ends someday. But eternity goes on for . . . well, eternity. That's where you want to be—in the right place—with God. And the only way to God is through our Savior Jesus Christ. "For all have sinned and fall short of the glory of God, and all are justified freely by His grace through the redemption that came by Jesus Christ" (Rom. 3:23).

Accept Him today and you're assured of eternity. The life of a Christian is not easy. It doesn't mean your troubles end and you float on a cloud all day. Sometimes it gets worse, but most times it's just great. The difference is that you've got God on your side for the remainder of your journey on this side of eternity.

Life with Christ is fun, exciting, challenging, as well as fulfilling and rewarding.

I invite you to, please, accept Jesus today by saying this prayer:

Lord Jesus, I realize that I'm a sinner. I come to You today to ask that You forgive me of all my sins and cleanse me of all unrighteousness. Come into my heart today and be my Lord and Savior.

If you said this prayer and mean it from you heart, voila! You're now a born-again child of God. You need to find and join a Bible-believing church in your area. You need to grow by being fed with the Word of God.

Congratulations!

AFTERWORD

FINI?

No, not yet.

This journal is the first in a series of my Inspirational Journals. The next installment will follow close on the heels of *Petals of Grace*. Interestingly, I was wrapping up my work on this book when the Lord dropped it in my heart to write a sort of sequel. I have already started work on it and hope it will be out in the next year. I trust you will follow me as I embark on another journey of hope, trust, faith, and love.

By the way, I am thrilled with the opportunity of meeting and connecting with my readers. A review of my book would be good, but it's not an absolute must. An email would be great, most definitely.

Here's where I hang out online:

Website: http://solamacaulay.com
Blog: http://thotsandmoments.com
Twitter: @olusolamac
Facebook: https://www.facebook.com/pages/Sola-Macaulay/533202360119403
Pinterest: http://www.pinterest.com/solamac/
GooglePlus: https://plus.google.com/117651201998967179616/posts
Email: sola@solamacaulay.com

I would love to hear from you. Perhaps you'd like me to pray for you. Maybe you need encouragement or you just want to say hello. I'm an email away.

Thanks so much for reading.
God's blessings!

Made in the USA
Charleston, SC
22 July 2015